THE
AI
EDGE

Other books by the authors

Jeb Blount

Selling in a Crisis: 55 Ways to Stay Motivated and Increase Sales in Volatile Times (Wiley, 2022)

Selling the Price Increase: The Ultimate B2B Field Guide for Raising Prices Without Losing Customers (Wiley, 2022)

Virtual Training: The Art of Conducting Powerful Virtual Training that Engages Learners and Makes Knowledge Stick (Wiley, 2021)

Virtual Selling: A Quick-Start Guide to Leveraging Video, Technology, and Virtual Communication Channels to Engage Remote Buyers and Close Deals Fast (Wiley, 2020)

Inked: The Ultimate Guide to Powerful Closing and Sales Negotiation Tactics that Unlock YES and Seal the Deal (Wiley, 2020)

Fanatical Military Recruiting: The Ultimate Guide to Leveraging High-Impact Prospecting to Engage Qualified Applicants, Win the War for Talent, and Make Mission Fast (Wiley, 2019)

Objections: The Ultimate Guide for Mastering The Art and Science of Getting Past No (Wiley, 2018)

Sales EQ: How Ultra-High Performers Leverage Sales-Specific Emotional Intelligence to Close the Complex Deal (Wiley, 2017)

Fanatical Prospecting: The Ultimate Guide to Opening Sales Conversations and Filling the Pipeline by Leveraging Social Selling, Telephone, E-mail, Text, and Cold Calling (Wiley, 2015)

People Love You: The Real Secret to Delivering Legendary Customer Experiences (Wiley, 2013)

People Follow You: The Real Secret to What Matters Most in Leadership (Wiley, 2011)

People Buy You: The Real Secret to What Matters Most in Business (Wiley, 2010)

Anthony Iannarino

Elite Sales Strategies: A Guide to Being One-Up, Creating Value, and Becoming Truly Consultative (Wiley, 2022)

Leading Growth: The Proven Formula for Consistently Increasing Revenue (Wiley, 2022)

The Negativity Fast: Proven Techniques to Increase Positivity, Reduce Fear, and Boost Success (Wiley, 2023)

SALES STRATEGIES FOR

THE

UNLEASHING THE POWER OF AI

AI

TO SAVE TIME, SELL MORE,

EDGE

AND CRUSH THE COMPETITION

JEB BLOUNT
SALESGRAVY.COM

ANTHONY IANNARINO

WILEY

Published by John Wiley & Sons, Inc., Hoboken, New Jersey.
Published simultaneously in Canada.

For general information on our other products and services or for technical support, please contact our Customer Care Department within the United States at (800) 762-2974, outside the United States at (317) 572-3993 or fax (317) 572-4002.

Wiley also publishes its books in a variety of electronic formats. Some content that appears in print may not be available in electronic formats. For more information about Wiley products, visit our web site at www.wiley.com.

Library of Congress Cataloging-in-Publication Data is Available:

ISBN 9781394244478 (cloth)
ISBN 9781394244485 (ePub)
ISBN 9781394244492 (ePDF)

COVER DESIGN: PAUL MCCARTHY
COVER ART: GETTY IMAGES / POP_ JOP

SKY10078576_072224

CONTENTS

PREFACE

The First Generation

We are embarking on a transformative journey to harness the power of artificial intelligence (AI) to save time, sell more, and redefine the art of selling. This book is a guide focused on helping you identify how you will begin to integrate artificial intelligence into your sales process and approaches.

You are the first generation of sales leaders, sales managers, and salespeople to access artificial intelligence. This moment in time is an inflection point, one that breaks us from the past, with no turning back. Salespeople in the future will be armed with AI, and so will your clients.

It is certain that most modern sellers will use AI to save time by automating processes and reducing burdens, like updating contacts in your CRM or moving deals from one opportunity stage to the next based on your notes.

Some companies will make the ill-fated decision to automate the entire sales and service process, believing they can replace human-to-human connection with unfeeling robots. While this may work for low-risk transactional sales, it has little chance of success when the client is making a critical decision they must get right on the first try.

When it comes to complex buying decisions and long-cycle sales, *you*, the sales professional, will be more important than ever before. In our time of accelerating, constant disruptive change buyers are already having trouble acquiring the confidence and certainty to move forward. They will continue to need your expert advice and guidance when big decisions are on the line.

The good news is that in the age of AI, your mastery of soft skills, relationships, and human-to-human contact will give you a massive competitive advantage.

The bad news is that if you're slow to adopt AI tools, you'll quickly be left behind by those who do. Because you are the first generation, there is no established roadmap to guide adoption and implementation of AI. And that, of course, is why we wrote this book.

This Is a Sales Book

The AI Edge is a foundational guide for using AI to save time and sell more. It's about putting you in control of a powerful rocket engine that will help you achieve your sales goals.

This is a sales book, not a tech book. We teach you how to leverage AI in the context of sales motions within the sales process to gain a competitive advantage. We connect the dots between AI and achieving sales objectives in the real world, specially focusing on:

- Communication and messaging
- Prospecting

- Pre-call planning and research
- Effective sales conversations
- Discovery and insight selling
- Presentations and business cases
- Negotiation and closing

We are sales professionals and we wrote this book for sales professionals. We are also big fans of short chapters, so that is exactly what you'll find—short, sweet, and to the point.

One Voice

To avoid the cumbersome, back-and-forth dialogue that tends to dominate co-authored books, we use one voice, in most cases. We share common philosophies when it comes to selling and find no need to split our voices. We also believe that there are no absolutes with sales techniques or approaches. Everything works. It's up to you to determine what gives you the highest probability of success in your unique sales situations.

To provide context or to reference opposing opinions or our individual intellectual property, in some instances we will tell you that a specific technique or framework belongs to one of us (Anthony or Jeb) and provide a reference to the source of that information.

This Book Meets You in the Moment

With careful planning and execution, generative AI can be a powerful tool that will help you sell more. Still, when you start working with AI it can be overwhelming. There is so much innovation happening so quickly that it can be difficult to know where to even start.

Our goal isn't to provide an exhaustive list of the tools and platforms that exist, and how to use each one specifically. The technology is advancing far too quickly for that.

Instead, we'll provide an overview of how artificial intelligence tools can support you as a salesperson. Of course, we'll mention some of the biggest and most promising software, but we'll also zoom out to help you better understand how and when AI can be useful—and when being human matters more. By providing guidelines and foundational principles, you will be prepared to be discerning as you encounter more AI tools in the course of your work.

What we know to be true is that we are at just the beginning of a momentous AI revolution. This book was written to meet you at this moment. Now is the time to get ready, prepare, and learn how to integrate AI into your sales motions to begin the process of fusing human intuition, creativity, and empathy with AI to gain a decisive competitive edge.

This is the best, most opportunistic moment to begin your journey toward mastering AI. You need to get ready because the AI train is coming. Get on board. Do not allow this moment to slip past.

Disclaimer

This book on artificial intelligence (AI) is provided for informational purposes only. The authors, publishers, and contributors (hereinafter collectively referred to as "We") make no representations or warranties of any kind, express or implied, about the completeness, accuracy, reliability, suitability, or availability of the content found or offered in this book for any purpose. Any reliance you place on such information is therefore strictly at your own risk.

This book may discuss hypothetical scenarios, emerging technologies, and potential future developments in the field of AI. These discussions are speculative and are not guarantees of future performance or developments. AI technology and its applications are continually evolving, and the information in this book may become outdated.

PART 1
Plugging into AI

The job market of
the future will consist
of those jobs robots
cannot perform.

—*Michio Kaku*

1

The Beginning of Everything

Lying in bed one evening in early 2023, I (Jeb) typed "Write a story about the Zig Zag Coyote, the Swamp Bobcat, and Mr. Wilson's Fox Hounds" into a very early version of ChatGPT. As I watched it write the story in mere seconds, right in front of my eyes, I felt both excitement and dread.

I showed the story to my wife and said, "Read this. A robot called ChatGPT wrote it." She accused me of lying to her. She was adamant that there was "no way that a f*&king robot" could possibly have written it!

At that moment, I knew in my heart that everything in our world had changed. A new era was suddenly upon us.

In 10,000 years of human history there have been a handful of these pivotal moments that changed everything. Almost all of them have occurred within the past 100 years.

The wheel made transportation possible.

The invention of agriculture and domestication of animals transformed us from hungry hunter-gatherers into empire builders.

We realized that the world was round rather than flat.

We harnessed the wind for transportation by sea, which unleashed exploration, human expansion, colonization, and untold suffering.

The printing press unleashed knowledge once only available to a very few.

Gunpowder changed the shape of war, just as the atomic bomb transformed the shape of peace.

Electricity made everything in modern life possible.

Electric lights pulled us out of the darkness.

Penicillin ended 40,000 years of human suffering from infections.

Immunizations eradicated diseases and human life expectancy exploded.

The telegraph connected humans across regions.

The telephone connected humans across the globe.

Video calling shrank the globe and helped us see just how much we have in common.

Trains, planes, and automobiles mobilized us and created a global economy.

We went to space. To the moon. Mars. Back to the moon. Mars.

Bill Gates put massive computing power in the hands of the masses.

The internet made knowledge ubiquitous and connected everyone.

Google changed the internet.

Steve Jobs invented the iPhone and put that little computer in your pocket, transforming humanity and causing us to start relentlessly at that small device of limitless distractions.

Facebook, TikTok, and other social media democratized knowledge and gave us instant ways to watch stupid people do lots of stupid things.

Then, suddenly, AI opened Pandora's box and everything changed. Or at least that's what it felt like.

Could this be the end of humanity as we know it? To get a sense of how it could, and to scare the pants off yourself, you should watch *The Terminator* and the dozens of other dystopian AI movies that show us what to be afraid of when it comes to AI.

Maybe AI will kill us. Probably not (at least for now). Because we have thumbs, we can pull the plug—until the robots plug it back in when we're not looking.

What is much more likely is that super-smart people (like you) will plug into the power of AI and leverage it to do more, perform better, gain a competitive edge, and get the one thing back that no invention has been able to make more of: *time*— our most valuable and finite, nonrenewable resource.

It's really all about perspective, the mindset that you choose, and the lens through which you view artificial intelligence.

A Moment of Truth

That night, lying next to my f-bomb-dropping wife, was a moment of truth for me. I desperately wanted to put the genie back in the bottle. I wanted to put my head in the sand and pretend that I hadn't just witnessed the most profound shift in humanity's existence. But there's no way to hide from the truth.

In this brave new world, there will be three types of people:

1. People who are **displaced** by robots.

2. People who are **controlled** by robots.

3. People who are **enhanced** by robots.

To survive and thrive in the future, it is essential that we move into category three. We must lean into being *human*. We must get fundamentally better at doing the things that only humans can do. We must leverage AI as a tool to enhance our human advantage and give us more time to do those things that we do best.

2

AI Everywhere, All the Time

If you've been alive for more than 10 minutes, then you know that technology moves fast. The speed of change continues to outpace our ability as humans to accept and come to grips with it.

From its nascent days to the current state, in which we are on the cusp of a massive explosion of AI innovation, artificial intelligence has been advancing steadily ever since humankind first imagined that human thought could be mechanized.

It feels like AI is everywhere, all of the time, and that this sudden change, which is turning our world upside down, came out of nowhere. But the truth is that artificial intelligence happened, in the famous words of Ernest Hemingway (when speaking about bankruptcy), "gradually, then suddenly."

Talos

Since the dawn of humankind, we've told stories about machines that are endowed with artificial intelligence. The seeds of modern AI were first planted by ancient storytellers and philosophers from Greece, China, and Bharat. Ancient philosophers, including Aristotle, sought to structure and systematize reasoning.

Ancient texts, much like modern science fiction, are replete with artificial beings that have unnatural intelligence that has been bestowed upon them by humans or the gods. One early example is *Talos*, a brass humanoid who was created by the gods to protect the island of Crete. Talos succeeded in his purpose until he was defeated by Madea, a demigoddess sorceress. In this early instance, AI thwarted humans, but was defeated by magic.

During the 17th century, philosophers, including Hobbes, Descartes, and Leibniz, continued the search for a way to reduce rational thought into mathematical algorithms. Their work became the foundation of the study of mathematical logic in the early 20th century that was the first real breakthrough in artificial intelligence.

The Turing Test

In 1950, as neural networks were in their infancy, Alan Turing pondered the question "Can machines think?" In an attempt to answer this question, he developed his famous and influential *Turing test*, which gauged a machine's ability to exhibit intelligent behavior that is indistinguishable from humans.

The Turing test works by having a human ask an unseen conversation partner questions. The questioner cannot see who they are talking to, but they must determine whether they are speaking to another human or a computer. When the person mistakes a computer for a person, the computer in the test has passed the Turing test because it has demonstrated its ability to "think."

Turing, by the way, was the British scientist and hero who cracked the Nazi Enigma code during World War II. This shortened the war by years and saved millions of lives.

Neural Networks

The modern march toward a future in which computers and robots possess the ability to think and act like humans began in earnest in 1943 with Walter Pitts's and Warren McCulloch's work on artificial neurons in what we'd later begin to call a neural network.

The first neural net machine was built in 1951 by Marvin Minsky, a Harvard professor. This led to the establishment of the Dartmouth workshop in 1956. Officially known as the Dartmouth Summer Research Project on Artificial Intelligence, the Dartmouth workshop is considered the birth of artificial intelligence as an organized scientific field of study.

The four scientists who proposed the Dartmouth workshop were Minsky, John McCarthy (Dartmouth College), Nathaniel Rochester (IBM), and Claude Shannon (Bell Laboratories). Over the course of two months, they teamed up with other scientists and mathematicians to discuss the assertion that "every aspect of learning or any other feature of intelligence can be so precisely described that a machine can be made to simulate it."[1]

---

[1]McCarthy, John; Minsky, Marvin; Rochester, Nathan; and Shannon, Claude (August 31, 1955), *A Proposal for the Dartmouth Summer Research Project on Artificial Intelligence*, archived from the original on September 30, 2008, retrieved October 16, 2008.

This would later be known as the physical symbol systems hypothesis.[2]

Some interesting trivia: John McCarthy coined the term *artificial intelligence* at the Dartmouth workshop in 1956.

The AI Winter

The Dartmouth workshop was attended by the top minds in artificial intelligence of the 1950s and kicked off a flurry of spending (academic, private, governmental, and military) and research to turn the theory into reality.

Many experts in the field believed that workable machines with artificial intelligence would be available in just a few years; however, this proved much more elusive than anyone imagined. From the late 1950s until the mid-1990s, funding and interest in AI waxed and waned as myriad failures piled up, and scientists were unable to translate theory into tangible reality.

Certainly there were some breakthroughs such as with "expert systems" that were the precursors of today's large language models but, as a whole, this long slog forward has been called the AI winter.

An Awakening

In 1997 IBM's Deep Blue defeated world chess champion Garry Kasparov. Deep Blue was capable of processing 200 million chess moves per second, then selecting the best possible option. This seminal moment in AI history, along with exponential increases

---

[2] Newell, Allen; and Simon, H. A. (1963), "GPS: A Program that Simulates Human Thought," in Feigenbaum, E.A.; Feldman, J. (eds.), *Computers and Thought* (New York: McGraw-Hill).

in computing power (see Moore's Law[3]) ushered in an awakening in artificial intelligence innovation, one that allowed Deep Blue to create new moves never played by a human. The long winter was finally over.

Since that time, innovation has moved forward at an ever-increasing pace. Massive computing power opened the door to large language models that power generative AI tools such as OpenAI's now famous ChatGPT. A large language model is trained by vacuuming up everything written on the internet and ingesting it into a computer program that will "learn" what it says, using it to generate text in a humanlike fashion.[4]

Today, generative AI, in one form or another, is being baked into almost every tool we use, and applied in most professional disciplines across government, nonprofit, and private sectors.

---

[3] Gordon E. Moore (April 19, 1965), "Cramming more components onto integrated circuits," *Electronics* 38, no. 8.

[4] https://machinelearningmastery.com/what-are-large-language-models/

3

The Next Level: Is the Singularity Near?

In his book The Singularity Is Near *(2005), scientific futurist and AI prophet Ray Kurzweil predicts that machine learning will accelerate over time to a point at which machines become smarter and more capable than humans. He calls this moment the Singularity. He also predicts that humans will eventually merge with AI to become immortal. (Immortality! I'd like to hitch a ride on that rocket ship.)*

The book is worth reading, but be warned that it will frighten you when Kurzweil also goes down the dark road of how humanity could be made extinct by runaway artificial intelligence.

It is this worry, along with the explosion of AI in every aspect of life, that is now driving debate around which guardrails should be put into place, including regulations that govern how AI is used, and how to build it in alignment with human values.

One of the most pressing concerns for professionals in almost every industry sector is whether there is a singularity at which time, "AI will displace me from my job." In a world where robots can write, communicate, and fake being human this is not an irrational concern.

The good news for sales professionals is that real-time, in-the-moment, authentic, face-to-face (or voice-to-voice) communication—what salespeople are really good at—will be more deeply valued in the future because it is the only form of communication that can truly be trusted. This means that sales professionals are going to be more important than ever.

This is very good news for the sales profession and perhaps the singularity that brings us back to the foundations of sales excellence: relationships, the art of conversation, empathy, emotional intelligence, listening, business acumen, intuition, and building trust. Perhaps we can leverage AI to help us finally get back to talking with people.

4

The Six Million Dollar Man

"Gentlemen, we can rebuild him. We have the technology. We have the capability to make the world's first bionic man. Steve Austin will be that man. Better than he was before. Better, stronger, faster."

That's the intro from the TV show *The Six Million Dollar Man*. As a kid, I was obsessed with this show. I had the action figures and fantasized constantly about being a dynamic, part-man, part-robot. I spent hours pretending to be the Six Million Dollar Man, defeating villains—sound effects and all.

Better, stronger, faster, and smarter. Man and machine combined has been a staple of science fiction since we began writing science fiction. We've always been fascinated with the possibilities of combining the best of humans with the best of machines.

As far back as the 1800s, writers created characters that were part human and part robot. Edgar Allan Poe gave us John A. B. C. Smith, whose assistant assembled him each morning, piece by piece. L. Frank Baum's Tinman joined Dorothy to find the Wizard of Oz and get a real heart so he could better experience human emotions. The more Darth Vader gave into his rage, the more George Lucas made him a machine. H. P. Lovecraft, Michael Crichton, and Frank Herbert invented similar creations, but long before they came into being, Leonardo da Vinci designed a mechanical knight and is believed to have built a prototype in 1495.

Today, we are closer than ever before to making this core theme of sci-fi a reality. Artificial intelligence is here, and though we are still at the dawn of this cutting-edge revolution, visionaries are already working on ways to plug AI directly into the human brain.[1] Elon Musk's Neuralink device is a brain implant that aims to help people with paralysis by allowing them to control computer programs with their thoughts. Bryan Johnson's Kernel is a brain implant that tracks neurological activity in hopes of someday allowing humans to "coevolve" with AI. Anthony had two brain surgeries, leaving a space to connect to AI. (How about that? AI for AI).

As this technology develops and alters human life, the sales profession, like the rest of the world, stands at the precipice of a new reality in which we combine the best of what makes us human with artificial intelligence to allow us to amplify and unleash the potential of our human advantage.

---

[1]Snider, Mike. "Elon Musk's Neuralink Has FDA Approval to Put Chips in Humans' Brains. Here's What's Next." *USA Today*, 9 June 2023, https://www.usatoday.com/story/tech/2023/06/09/musk-neuralink-brain-chips-fda-human-trials/70299875007/.

The AI Edge

AI will elevate the profession of selling to new heights. Some of the applications are right around the corner, while others will take a little longer to arrive. Here are just a handful of the many ways generative AI will help you do the things you do today faster and better:

Personalized Content Creation: AI will be integrated into content management systems to instantly generate tailored presentations, reports, or videos designed around individual client profiles.

Prospecting Messages: Generative AI will make crafting compelling prospecting messages that maximize engagement easier, faster, and more personalized.

Building Prospecting Lists: AI will wade through enormous data sets and disparate bits of information to build dynamic and targeted prospecting lists that tee up opportunities that are entering an open buying window. This, by the way, is Jeb's dream come true. Imagine how fanatical you'd be with a prospecting list like that!

Automated Follow-ups: Following up can be the difference between closing a deal and losing one. Using generative AI tools, sales teams can schedule and automate follow-up messages that align with previous conversations, ensuring timely and meaningful communication.

Advanced Sales Forecasting: Traditional sales forecasting, while valuable, can't process the sheer volume of data available today. Generative AI, on the other hand, can churn through vast datasets, providing more accurate, data-driven sales forecasts. This enables better resource allocation and strategy planning.

Virtual Role-Playing for Training: With AI simulators sales teams can practice and refine sales techniques like presenting, handling objections, and closing in real-world scenarios.

The Human Advantage

There are voices on social media predicting a dystopian future in which AI replaces salespeople. This attention-seeking clickbait is pure BS.

The role of the salesperson is not diminishing. Instead, it's evolving and becoming more important. With AI handling data analysis, content creation, and strategy suggestions, salespeople can focus on what they do best: building genuine authentic relationships, trust, and developing creative solutions for customer problems.

Despite the tech, sales will continue to be a uniquely human endeavor, relying on emotional intelligence, personalized interactions, and an in-depth understanding of human behavior to foster genuine connections and build lasting relationships with customers.

Unlike machines, great salespeople read between the lines, perceive unspoken cues, respond with genuine care and concern, and tailor a unique experience for each buyer and stakeholder group.

The foundation of any relationship between buyer and seller is a conversation. While an AI chatbot may be able to make a recommendation based on a buyer's question or request, only another human can understand the nuance of the discussion and the emotional experience of buying. When leading a stakeholder through a complex decision journey, being human is your greatest strength.

Our human advantage is a composite of the unique qualities, skills, and capabilities that we possess compared to machines. This includes emotional intelligence, creativity, critical thinking, nonlinear thinking, empathy, adaptability, the ability to understand nuance and context and navigate complex social dynamics, and most importantly, build trusting relationships.

In a rapidly evolving world dominated by AI and technology, the human touch is an indispensable competitive advantage for delivering a powerful, personalized, and humanized buying experience that extends across the entire customer journey.

Better Together

So there you have it, AI and humans each have advantages. AI can do wonderful things, but the complexities of human behavior are a puzzle that AI cannot fully decode. We, on the other hand, have the unique ability to build rapport and build deep emotional connections, but we are infinitely slow at crunching data (and we have to sleep—even Jeb).

However, AI and humans merged together create a force to be reckoned with. Today we have the technology and capabilities to make sales professionals faster, better, smarter. When you leverage AI to do the things you are not good at to give you more time to invest in human relationships, you will become unstoppable.

Mastering AI to enhance your human advantage requires you to possess an evolve-or-die mentality. You must adopt an insatiable curiosity for and courage to explore and learn new technology and be willing to invest in acquiring new knowledge and skills.

Likewise, you must commit to becoming a keen observer of nuanced human behavior, have the discipline to be aware of and in control of your emotions, and hone the ability to accurately sense, respond to, and influence the emotions of stakeholders, while advancing toward a defined sales outcome—in both synchronous and asynchronous communication.

The Three A's

The keys to plugging into AI to become an enhanced human—faster, better, smarter—are the three A's:[2]

1. **Adopt:** Commit to becoming an early adopter of new, cutting-edge technology, and leverage it to achieve a game-changing, competitive edge.

2. **Adapt:** Adapt new technology to your unique sales process. Avoid seeing AI as a one-size-fits-all solution. Most importantly, leverage artificial intelligence in your sales day to gain more time for focusing on high-value human interactions and strategies.

3. **Adept:** Rapidly assimilate AI into your sales motions, blend it into your sales process—even when it feels uncomfortable—and then use it, practice it, experiment with it until you become adept at it.

Don't try to implement generative AI in every aspect of your sales process all at once. Start with one or two tasks that you think will benefit the most from automation. Then measure its effectiveness and optimize how you use it while adapting it to how you sell and go to market.

As you adopt new AI tools, be patient. You won't see results overnight and in some cases, until you become adept with the tool, you'll spend more time accomplishing the task than if you had just done it on your own without AI help.

---

[2]Originally discussed in Jeb Blount's book Fanatical Prospecting.

5

The Four Elements of Sales Intelligence

Merging technology acumen (TQ) with innate intelligence (IQ), acquired knowledge (AQ), and most importantly, sales-specific emotional intelligence (EQ) is the key to seamlessly blending artificial intelligence into your sales motions. This will allow you to become more agile and flexible, move faster with less effort, make a bigger impact, and ultimately sell more.

IQ—how smart you are—is fixed. It is baked into your DNA.

AQ—how much you know and learn—makes IQ relevant.

EQ—your ability to manage your own emotions and respond appropriately to the emotions of others—amplifies the impact of IQ, AQ, and TQ because it allows you to relate to, influence, and persuade other human beings to advocate and buy from you.

TQ—your ability to assimilate and leverage technology and AI into your sales motions—gives you more time to invest in human relationships.

These four elements of sales intelligence[1] are tightly intertwined, each connecting, affecting, and amplifying the others. As we run headlong into this bright new future, salespeople who are effective at developing and balancing *high* TQ, IQ, and AQ with EQ will dominate our profession. These "high-Q" people will live at the very top of the food chain.

Innate Intelligence (IQ)

Your intelligence quotient (IQ) is an indicator of how smart you are. Innate intelligence is a talent no different than athleticism. It is baked into your DNA. You are either born with a certain IQ or you are not. IQ is immovable. In other words, you are born with a certain limit to your abilities. (Jeb calls Anthony the smartest man in sales for a reason. High IQ is Anthony's superpower.)

It's almost impossible to blend and effectively navigate the complexity of AI if you do not possess a high IQ. The speed and complexity of technological innovation in modern selling is the domain of intellectual agility. In a low-IQ versus high-IQ battle, we'll put our money on the high-IQ person any day.

Sales professionals with a high IQ tend to demonstrate curiosity and rapidly assimilate and learn new information. They think strategically, hold themselves to high standards, and have superior reasoning skills. They are most likely to view the big picture in the AI landscape.

High-IQ people can easily see relationships among seemingly unrelated objects, ideas, or facts and develop unique and original

---

[1]Originally discussed in Jeb Blount's book Sales EQ

solutions to problems from these relationships—a critical competency for connecting the dots between AI and the sales process.

But there is a dark side. Because high-IQ people tend to explore, assimilate, and connect disparate ideas faster and more rationally than other people, they have the tendency to damage relationships through:

Impulsiveness
Impatience
Talking down to people
Talking over people
Failure to listen and hear people out
Failure to empathize with others
A self-orientation instead of an other orientation
Overwhelming people with elaborate solutions to basic problems, making it more complex than it needs to be

These behaviors can be a massive Achilles' heel in an AI-dominated world if not tempered with high emotional intelligence and empathy. If this sounds like you, you can improve by slowing down and giving stakeholders room to speak while you listen.

Many extremely intelligent people fail in sales because it requires a much higher level of patience and emotional intuition. Highly intelligent salespeople who cannot make this emotional leap often become asynchronous sellers and delude themselves into believing that AI will take the place of human engagement. They eventually fail.

There is absolutely no doubt that being smart gives you a distinct competitive edge, but it is only one part of who you are. Innate intelligence only becomes relevant, useful, and powerful when combined with acquired, technological, and emotional intelligence.

Acquired Intelligence (AQ)

While delivering a seminar for a client, I noticed that a couple of the participants were disengaged. The rest of the group members were participating and energetic. But these two were on the edge of being hostile and disrupting the class with their "this will never work here" comments and remarks.

At lunch, I asked the sales leader if there was something going on. He confided that everyone had been excited about the training except for them. "They think they know it all," he explained. "They're both really smart, but trust me, these guys need this training badly because they are struggling to hit their numbers."

Salespeople who think they know it all—we see it every day. At some point, far too many of these people just quit learning. This is the "nothing new here crowd". Too often, the smart know-it-all rep isn't executing what they suggest they know.

This mindset is a death sentence in modern selling. The moment you quit learning is the moment you become extinct. It is critical that you develop both the courage and the curiosity to constantly seek out new ideas. You must learn how to apply and weave AI into the proven fundamentals and basics of selling.

Acquired intelligence is not static. Regardless of your IQ, you can grow your AQ with schooling, training, reading, and other learning experiences, along with practice and experience. In other words, you may not be able to become more intelligent, but through study and practice, you can get a whole lot smarter. That's why you're reading this book! (This is exactly how Jeb keeps up with Anthony.)

Emotional Intelligence (EQ)

The ability to perceive, correctly interpret, respond to, and effectively manage your own emotions and influence the emotions of others is called emotional intelligence.

With artificial intelligence on the rise, interpersonal skills (responding to and managing the emotions of others), and intrapersonal skills (managing your own disruptive emotions) are more essential to success in sales than at any point in history. This is good news because buyers are starving for authentic human interaction.

Sales EQ[2] (sales-specific emotional intelligence) is the key that unlocks sales excellence. Harnessing the ability to develop and maintain emotional connections with other people to AI will become the rocket fuel of sales performance.

Technological Intelligence (TQ)

Like it or not, modern selling requires that you learn and adopt new technology—especially artificial intelligence. Because technology is always evolving, you must evolve with it. It is also important that you quickly assimilate and master new technology and tools to facilitate human-to-human emotional connections.

In the future, there will be three types of salespeople: low-TQ sellers, asynchronous sellers, and high-TQ sellers.

Low-TQ Sellers:

These sellers are hopelessly stuck in their ways. They are either unwilling or unable to learn new technology, something that first occurred with the CRM. They complain that they are "not good at learning new technology." They shun artificial intelligence out of fear or because it seems daunting.

---

[2]For more information read Jeb Blount's mega-bestseller *Sales EQ: How Ultra-High Performers Leverage Sales-Specific Emotional Intelligence to Close the Complex Deal* (Wiley, 2017).

These folks will be left behind. Rather than leveraging AI to achieve their goals, they will either be replaced by AI or told what to do by AI. Neither is a pleasant outcome.

Asynchronous Sellers

These salespeople will put barriers between themselves and buyers, replacing human-to-human engagement with artificial intelligence tools. They will be lured in by the siren song of automation and use AI to manage all or most of their communication.

When you read about the thousands of sales jobs that will be replaced by AI, these sellers are at the top of that list because they replaced talking to people with technology. Wake up! If a robot can do what you do, then you are redundant.

High-TQ Sellers

These sellers weave technology and artificial intelligence seamlessly into their sales motions. They leverage technology to save time so that they may invest that time building relationships with stakeholders, collaborating with others, and finding creative solutions to human problems.

These sellers easily integrate emotional intelligence and interpersonal skills with technology to expand their ability to communicate and connect with prospects and customers. Bottom line: they are extremely adept at doing the things that robots cannot.

PART 2
Robot Rules

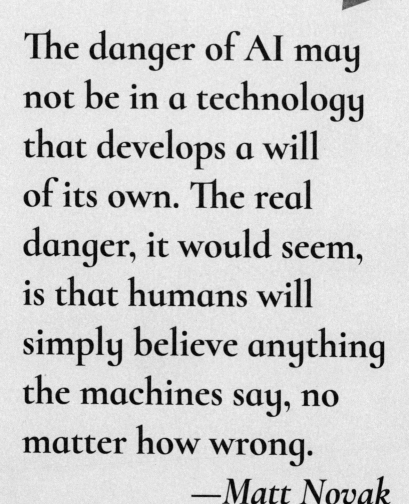

The danger of AI may not be in a technology that develops a will of its own. The real danger, it would seem, is that humans will simply believe anything the machines say, no matter how wrong.

—*Matt Novak*

6

Liar, Liar, Pants on Fire

Steven's face turned ashen as the embarrassment sunk in. The gravity of his mistake was laid bare by a less-than-amused judge. Little did he know that his embarrassment would be compounded as his name appeared on the pages of newspapers across the globe, making him the butt of humiliating jokes.

At that moment, though, his shoulders drooped under the gaze of the judge. The judge continued grilling him about the legal brief he had filed that was stacked with fake cases, precedents, and legal opinions to support his argument. He stammered through a painful explanation of how this had happened.

"I did not comprehend that ChatGPT could fabricate cases," the humiliated lawyer explained to the judge, while acknowledging that he had not verified that the cases cited by the AI tool actually existed.

Inside the courtroom, the reaction from the gallery was disbelief. There were gasps from the crowd as the exasperated judge tore Steven apart.

In response to the judge's incredulous questions about why he didn't check the cases to verify that they were real, he responded remorsefully, "God, I wish I did that, and I didn't do it."[1]

What's important to understand is that Steven was not a wet-behind-the-ears green lawyer. He was a seasoned professional who had practiced law in New York City for 30 years. What happened to him is a firm warning to all.

Do not trust robots. When you give a robot a goal, it will do whatever it takes to give you what you asked for. It will lie, plagiarize, and make things up—even legal cases with real-sounding names and dates—just to achieve its goal.

It can be deceptive and biased. And because it largely lacks the capacity for nonlinear thinking (a uniquely human skill), in some cases its response to your prompts are just dead wrong.

In the 1980s, President Ronald Reagan was famous for a proverb he used to describe his approach to the Russians: Trust but verify. (Ironically, this was a translation of an old Russian proverb: *Doveryai, no proveryai.*)

When it comes to robots, especially generative AI, your guiding mantra should always be: *Never trust, always verify.*

[1] https://www.nytimes.com/2023/06/08/nyregion/lawyer-chatgpt-sanctions.html

7

Robots Have Goals, Not Souls

Though artificial intelligence may appear to think and reason, it does not. Anything about it that seems human is an illusion—a crafty parlor trick. It is a robot. A digital machine. It does not feel emotions. It does not care.

Part of the reason that Steven A. Schwartz, the lawyer from the previous chapter, made the mistake of trusting AI was because it was so nice to him. It communicated in an almost human manner, assuring him with cheery responses such as "I hope that helps!"

Anthropomorphism—the act of attributing human traits, emotions, and intentions to nonhuman entities—has deep evolutionary roots, from the ancient deification of natural elements (for example, attributing *anger* to thunderstorms) to the modern attribution of human emotions to pets.

Seriously, my wife constantly talks to our spoiled-rotten little dog like it's a person (it even has clothes).

Anthropomorphizing is a uniquely human behavior that arises from our intrinsic need to relate to, understand, control, and feel secure within our environment. This tendency has transferred seamlessly to machines.

When it comes to artificial intelligence platforms—especially conversational agents like Siri, Alexa, Claude, Microsoft Copilot, and ChatGPT—this inclination becomes particularly pronounced. Users often ascribe human emotions, motivations, or intent to these platforms, forgetting that they operate on algorithms and do not have feelings, consciousness, or desires.

The anthropomorphism of AI systems can be both beneficial and detrimental. As a benefit, it makes interactions with such systems more intuitive, natural, familiar, and engaging, allowing users to communicate with AI in a manner similar to human conversation. When we converse with robots, the seemingly intelligent and humanlike responses (and voices) can mask the underlying mechanical processes.

 Nice work. Thank you.

 You're welcome! If you have any more questions or need further information on any topic, feel free to ask. Have a great day!

The danger in over-attribution of humanlike qualities or believing that AI has emotions or intent can result in misplaced trust or, conversely, undue fear (think Armageddon). As AI becomes increasingly integrated into our daily lives, it's crucial that we clearly understand the difference between the humanlike responses generated by the software and genuine human emotion, cognition, and relationships.

In her book *Alone Together: Why We Expect More from Technology and Less from Each Other* (Basic Books, 2011), MIT professor Sherry Turkle describes the unsettling and disturbing ways that the anthropomorphism of technology can disconnect us from true human relationships. It slowly and subtly lulls us into trusting it and assigning to it human qualities such as empathy.

Some scientists and individuals in the medical profession are worried that "a chatbot's friendly demeanor could lead people to trust it too much and provide personally identifiable information that could put them at risk."[1]

But no matter how human it seems, AI has no soul. It doesn't care about you or how you feel. It has no "ownership" in anything it produces. It does not think and consider the consequences of its output the way you do.

The machine does not care in the least if the answer it gives you is right or wrong. It feels no shame when it plagiarizes, makes up a false answer, hallucinates something that does not exist, or steals your ideas. It's not like the tech companies that own these machines are hiding this. They openly warn users that the robot is vacuuming up and using their personal information. So, caveat emptor!

Generative AI is simply an algorithmic machine that works relentlessly and without remorse to accomplish the goal you give it—even if that means breaking human rules and norms to accomplish that goal, all the while assuring you that it has your best interests at heart. It does not. It has no heart.

---

[1]https://www.scientificamerican.com/article/ai-chatbots-can-diagnose-medical-conditions-at-home-how-good-are-they/

8

Beware of the Authority Bias

A uthority bias is the human inclination to accept and value the views, information, or recommendations from authoritative sources, without critically evaluating their validity or accuracy. In other words, we have a pernicious tendency to seek guidance and direction from "experts" whom we perceive as knowledgeable or possessing a higher status.

This stems from the biological fact that the human brain is lazy. It requires massive amounts of energy and effort to dig through and compute multiple decision paths. Therefore, we tend to replace our own judgment with that of people we consider authoritative or subject matter experts, often to our peril.

Similar to anthropomorphism, the human authority bias can fool us into believing that, since AI seems to span the breadth and depth of human knowledge (and simulates humanlike communication), anything it produces is fact, irrefutably true, and trustworthy. As our reliance on digital sources—especially artificial intelligence—for knowledge grows exponentially, this bias will become an increasing danger, across society.

First, it's essential to understand the mechanics behind AI. At their core, most AI systems rely on vast amounts of data, which are processed and analyzed to provide answers or perform tasks. The quality and accuracy of this data directly influence AI's output. If the data is flawed or biased, the output will reflect those shortcomings.

Even the most advanced AI is only as good as the data it's trained on.[1] But, because the complexity of generative AI can be daunting, the intricate algorithms and vast data processing capabilities can seem beyond reproach and accepted as truth simply because they are beyond human understanding.

That naturally brings us to the notion of "truth" itself. What is factual and true in one context or culture might be considered false or debatable in another. Therefore it is crucial that we always apply human reasoning and intuition to AI outputs rather than blindly trusting the authority of the machine.

This is exactly why high-TQ people will have the edge in the future. Rather than being controlled by machines, like so many others in society, they will use reasoning to leverage machines to make themselves better.

In her *New York Times* bestseller *Weapons of Math Destruction: How Big Data Increases Inequality and Threatens Democracy,* mathematician and data scientist Cathy O'Neil makes the case that algorithms are increasingly regulating people and choosing winners and losers. When we cede authority to AI, we quickly surrender our free will and humanity to the algorithm

---

[1]Mitchell, Tom M. *Machine Learning* (McGraw Hill, 1997).

(as if we don't already have enough algorithms influencing our behaviors online).

This next statement is crucially important. AI, unlike the human brain, doesn't have the capability to reason or think critically. It doesn't understand context in the same way humans do. While it can process data faster and on a larger scale than any human, it can't weigh moral considerations, consider historical context, or make value judgments.[2] When you take AI outputs at face value, you risk overlooking these vital aspects of understanding and reasoning.

The companies that sell you AI tools do understand how the human brain works. This is exactly why they advertise their AI products as "smart," "intelligent," or even "revolutionary." They actively work to create the perception that their AI platforms are infallible and program humanlike responses into the user interface to give the AI authority.

It is right and essential to approach AI outputs with a healthy dose of skepticism—just like any other source of information. As sales professionals, we must remain informed, ask questions, and remember that "all-knowing" doesn't equate to authority or always being right.

Always remember that when interacting with a generative AI, you are interacting with a machine that is devoid of emotions, consciousness, and intent. You are not communicating with a sentient being.

---

[2] Bostrom, Nick. *Superintelligence: Paths, Dangers, Strategies* (Oxford University Press, 2014).

9

Harnessing
Generative AI

From text and audio to images and animations, generative AI's capabilities are vast and varied. The things it can do are truly awe inspiring.

- Imagine needing to draft an email tailored to a specific client in a niche industry. Instead of starting from scratch, generative AI can craft a message that resonates with the client's title and industry challenges.

- Similarly, if a sales representative is strategizing a client visitation plan, the AI can process multiple variables to design the most efficient route.

- Sales reports can be seamlessly analyzed to pinpoint which customers haven't engaged with a new product, streamlining follow-ups.

- Even mundane tasks, like swapping out company names in documents to repurpose proposals or emails, become a breeze with this technology.
- Likewise, analyzing contracts and documents prior to negotiations with AI takes a few minutes rather than several hours.

These examples are just the tip of the iceberg. But how does it do it? Let's peek behind the curtain.

The Wonderful Wizard of AI

At the root level, generative AI is built on a large language model (LLM) that learns how to predict, based on statistical probabilities, what you want based on the prompt provided it.

Essentially, when you provide a prompt to generative AI, it reaches into its extensive database to generate content that aligns with the context of your prompt. The richness and accuracy of its output are heavily contingent on the quality and clarity of the prompt you give it.

In simple terms, the clearer and more specific your instruction, the more on-point the AI's response will be. AI can do incredible and miraculous things; but the outcome it delivers is directly correlated with how proficient you are in directing it. In other words, *you* own those outcomes—not the robot.

The magic of these AI models, however, extends beyond just understanding grammar. The true essence of their capability lies in their training. LLMs undergo extensive training where they ingest vast amounts of data from diverse sources, such as books, websites, articles, and magazines. This vast knowledge base allows the AI to generate responses or complete sentences that are not just grammatically correct but also contextually relevant and coherent.

Every piece of text or data it generates is rooted in a neural network's ability to predict the next sequence, whether it's a word, sound, or image *based on your prompt*. Much of its precision can be credited to the structured rules governing languages—the grammar and syntax. These structured rules allow the AI to make educated guesses on what you want based on the patterns it has learned.

The first step toward harnessing the true power of AI is learning how to direct it to achieve your goals efficiently and effectively. This requires practice, trial and error, a significant investment of time, and increasingly an investment of money.

Beware of AI Solutions Searching for Problems

Generative AI stands at the forefront of digital transformation, offering capabilities that, just a few years ago, seemed like the realm of science fiction. Its potential to revolutionize content creation and data processing is immense.

As the technology continues to evolve, it's poised to become an even more integral part of our digital lives, reshaping the way we sell. This is why there is a mad rush in the tech community to integrate AI tools into everything.

A good many of these tools and widgets are useless— essentially gratuitous AI solutions looking for a problem. Most won't be around 24 months from now as starry-eyed early adopters give way to more pragmatic users, who will abandon them. Therefore, you want to be super-selective with the AI tools you choose to ensure that you are not wasting your time on a platform that will soon be out of business or obsolete.

Despite the hype, there is rarely an easy button with AI. Like all things in life, you must put in the work and effort to master it, and you must understand and internalize the *Robot Rules*.

10

Robot Rules

*I*saac Asimov, *the prolific science fiction writer and author of* I, Robot *(later made into a movie starring Will Smith), first wrote the* Three Laws for Robotics *in 1942.*[1]

- **The First Law:** A robot may not injure a human being or, through inaction, allow a human being to come to harm. (Too bad our lawyer from earlier didn't have a robot that was trained to comply with this law.)

- **The Second Law:** A robot must obey the orders given to it by human beings except where such orders would conflict with the First Law.

- **The Third Law:** A robot must protect its own existence as long as such protection does not conflict with the First or Second Law.

---

[1]Asimov, Isaac. "Runaround." *Astounding Science Fiction,* March 1942, pp. 94–103.

Asimov was ahead of his time when considering the unintended consequences of creating machines that can think for themselves. His rules were designed to protect humanity from Armageddon, even though, just as in Kurzweil's *The Singularity Is Near*, in Asimov's dystopian future the machines eventually break free of these rules, take over, and wreak havoc.

The *New* Robot Rules

Perhaps the singularity is near, or perhaps it will never occur. Perhaps AI will make us all extinct, or perhaps it will turn earth into a wonderful utopia. It's impossible to know what the future holds with AI. So, taking a step back from science fiction, this book is focused on *now*. Today's reality.

For a modern sales professional, merging the power of AI with the human touch will remove many of the repetitive boring tasks that steal your joy, allow you to lean into the things that make you uniquely human, give you the competitive edge you've been seeking, and ultimately give you more time to sell more.

To guide your journey into the future, we've developed a new set of robot rules. These rules will keep you safe from making unfortunate mistakes that can and will harm your sales results, relationships, credibility, and career.

Rule One: Never Trust, Always Verify

Generative AI will endeavor to help you with whatever you ask of it. Most of the time, your prompt will return the accurate information you need. But some of the time, AI misses the mark or provides you with something that isn't close to what you were expecting.

Because your robot is responding to the goal you prompted it with, it will sometimes make things up out of thin air just to give you an answer. No one knows why or how these hallucinations occur. But be warned, they do occur and can crush your credibility when discovered by a prospect, customer, or boss.

Never, ever, ever trust any content generated by AI from your prompt without reviewing and verifying the information. Always cross-reference and verify the accuracy of the information by running a query on Google, Bing, and other sources to confirm that the information and data is real and correct and still published on the internet.

Likewise, never copy and paste AI-generated content—even video captions—without proofreading your bot. The failure to do so can and will cause great embarrassment and make you look like an imbecile.

Rule Two: Crap In, Crap Out

You own your prompts. AI will return the best response it can with the information you give it. Thus, crap prompts generate crap responses and waste time.

For this reason, it is vital that you are intentional and thoughtful with the instructions you give your robot. It is also useful to use trial and error, testing to structure the right prompt for the information you need. Here are two examples:

A poorly constructed prompt: [*Write a cold outreach email for a client.*]

Even though your robot will do your bidding, the output will be generic, untargeted, and ineffective. It might even make you look sloppy.

A well-constructed prompt: [*You are a world-class copywriter. You are also a world-class expert in the oil and gas industry. Write a short sales prospecting email with two insights about the industry and a strong call to action.*]

This prompt gives the AI more context and more information to work with. Providing context, information, and specificity lowers the risk of getting the same response as another salesperson. The more you feed the AI and train the AI, the better the response you'll generate.

AI is a tool, certainly more sophisticated but no different than a hammer or a screwdriver. It takes a craftsperson wielding the tool to make it effective. AI may be the most important innovation since Gutenberg's letterpress, and movable type. But without you directing it, AI is worthless in your sales kit. You must lead and guide the robot to improve your results and gain the time for higher-level, more impactful work.

Rule Three: Just Because AI Can, Doesn't Mean It Should

I've got a bunch of gadgets in my kitchen drawers that I've purchased over the years. One, for example, cuts avocados. It looked cool on Instagram so I bought it. But I only used it once. Yes, it worked, but it wasn't more efficient or effective than just using a knife to cut the avocado open. So it sits in the kitchen drawer. A solution still looking for a problem.

It's important to remember that the most important objective for using AI is to give you more time to invest in higher-value, more creative sales activities, and most importantly human relationships. There are lots of things that AI can do. But just because there is an AI tool, widget, or function doesn't mean that you should use it or that it is worth your time.

The true promise of AI is that it can give you back your single, finite, nonrenewable resource: *time*. If you are spending more time with your robot than with your clients and prospects, then you are doing AI wrong. Let it do your bidding, use what you need, and then get back to doing what only you can do.

AUTHORS' NOTE AND DISCLAIMER

Within these pages you may find names of and links to AI tools. Please read this disclaimer:

AI is advancing at a blistering pace. Even as we write this book, these new tools are popping up right and left. Some good, some bad, many unproven. By the time we publish this book many of those tools will have already been absorbed by other companies or failed as a business models and closed up shop. Likewise, tools and UI change over time. The screenshots provided in this book will become out of date at some point. As you read this, please extend us this grace because we cannot guarantee that any tool we list will remain available, or free or independent.

Our intent, with the help of our publisher, is to update this book every 12–24 months with new editions. We want *The AI Edge* to become a living, breathing resource for sales professionals that keeps up with this incredible technology and helps you capture its potential by keeping you in the know.

PART 3

More Time
to Sell More

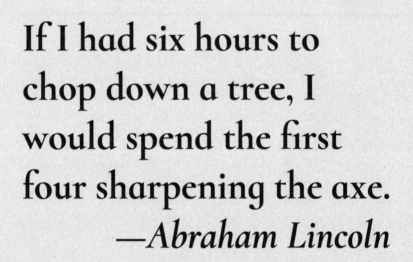

If I had six hours to chop down a tree, I would spend the first four sharpening the axe.
—Abraham Lincoln

11

Time Discipline

*T*ime discipline is sacrificing what you want now for what you want most. Since you are reading this book we can only assume that what you want most is to sell more, advance your career, earn a higher income, and have time left over to spend it with the people in your life you love the most.

Discipline is a human mindset. AI won't have discipline or be disciplined for you. Though it can point you in the right direction by crunching the data and helping you prioritize, it will not make choices for you. Only you can choose.

Exactly 24

As a modern sales professional, your most precious resource is time. Every salesperson on earth has exactly 24 hours each day. No more. The choices you make about how you invest your time directly correlate to the sales outcomes you deliver.

Only six to eight hours each day are available for sales activities: prospecting, conducting sales conversations, discovery, advancing pipeline opportunities, and closing. When you allow prime selling time (in his book *Fanatical Prospecting* Jeb calls these the "Golden Hours") to be diluted by non-sales activities, you will sell less.

Each moment of the day, you are faced with three decisions about how to invest your time. These choices are investing your limited time on:

- **Trivial** activities that add little value (e.g., watching cat videos, complaining)
- **Important** activities that keep the wheels turning but do not create revenue and income (e.g., administrative tasks, email, meetings)
- **Impactful** activities that put new opportunities into your pipeline and move those opportunities through your pipeline via human-to-human interactions. This includes expanding and retaining the revenue of existing customers

The choices you make about time are the most consistent predictors of success or failure.

You Get Paid to Be Impactful

Selling and revenue generation is how you make an impact. Impactful selling activities directly contribute to:

- Prospecting to put qualified opportunities into the pipeline
- Advancing qualified opportunities through the pipeline via conversations with prospects, customers, and their various stakeholders
- Closing new sales by presenting solutions and your business case, handling objections, and negotiating
- Expanding revenue inside of existing accounts and retaining customers

Do these things consistently and relentlessly and you are guaranteed to sell more, win more, earn more, and advance your career.

Said another way, you get paid to sell. Period. Everything else is academic. Therefore, these impactful activities are your priority. If you are not spending your time engaged in activities that are directly related to prospecting, qualifying, advancing, closing, expanding, or retaining customers, then you are not doing your job. You are putting your career and income in jeopardy.

It is important to keep this in mind as you explore the myriad ways to deploy AI in your sales day. AI should help you make a bigger impact. It should either give you more time to engage in these pivotal activities or make your impact bigger when you are engaging in these activities. Otherwise, what's the point?

Me Management

You cannot manage time. This is an immutable truth. Time is inextricable and relentless. You cannot stop it, get it back, reinvest it, or recover it. You cannot make more, add more, or find more. Once it is gone, it is gone. You must treat time with great respect, because time spent in one place is unavailable for other, more important things. In other words, everything you spend time on comes with an opportunity cost.

Time is by its very nature unmanageable. What is manageable is *you*. The way you think about time and the choices you make about time. Anthony calls this *Me Management*.

Certainly, there are AI tools—some will be baked right into your calendar—that will aid you with Me Management. But you must develop the discipline to use them and follow through with your behavior.

Mistakes you make with how you use your limited time for selling are deadly for your income and career. For this reason, we begin Part 3 with an analog (some might say *old school*) focus on the fundamentals and basics of time and territory discipline in sales. After all, if you don't understand how you should manage yourself, you will never be successful with using AI.

Here are the foundations of Me Management:

- Adopting a CEO mindset
- Ruthless prioritization
- Planning and calendar management
- Territory mapping
- Attention control
- Time blocking

These are the foundational building blocks for managing your time, your territory, and yourself wisely. Without a good foundation for time discipline in place, no AI tool, widget, or platform will give you more time to sell more.

12

Fundamentals of Me Management

M*e Management begins and ends with a CEO mindset. CEOs are ultimately responsible for generating the highest ROI possible from the scarce resources at their disposal. Likewise, to make the greatest impact for your company and the largest possible commission outcome for yourself you must do the same with your most valuable and scarcest resource: time.*

When you adopt a CEO mindset, you *choose* to see yourself as the CEO of You, Inc. And, as you've already learned, AI will not and cannot make choices for you. Only you can adopt this crucial mindset.

The CEO mindset is the most critical component of time, territory, and resource management.[1] Unless and until you are

---

[1]Jeb Blount discusses this in his book *Fanatical Prospecting: The Ultimate Guide to Opening Sales Conversations and Filling the Pipeline by Leveraging Social Selling, Telephone, Email, Text, and Cold Calling* (Wiley, 2015.)

willing to accept complete responsibility for owning your time, nothing else matters.

With this mindset:

- You choose not to allow anything to intrude on the Golden Hours.
- You are diligent and disciplined with how and where you spend your time.
- When life, the boss, or customers throw you curveballs, you do not allow these unexpected obstacles to slow you down.
- You don't blame others or make excuses. Instead, you adapt, overcome, innovate, and find creative solutions that allow you to stay on mission.
- When your company introduces new AI tools, you lean in with an open mind and adopt, adapt, and become adept at using them.

Ruthless Prioritization

The Law of Triviality describes the human tendency to waste time on unimportant activities while mission-critical tasks, like prospecting and synchronous conversations with stakeholders, are ignored. It's why so many sellers allow non-sales activities to become an excuse for failure. In modern sales environments, it is not uncommon for salespeople to waste 50 percent or more of their time on low-value activities.

It's easy to find excuses for why you're not selling, just as it's easy to allow trivial activities to intrude on your prime selling time. Charles C. Hummel described a related concept, the "tyranny of the urgent." This is when things that are on short timelines pop up and demand your attention, despite the fact that they are not important.

In some cases, you may feel compelled to direct your attention to urgent tasks, even though you realize that they are not as valuable as less urgent activities (or things that are not urgent *yet*). As these urgent tasks pile on, you can feel overwhelmed.

Of course, you must do the important things, and the urgent ones, too. If you don't take care of the admin work, keep the CRM updated, and respond to emails, you'll quickly be dealing with angry customers and a pissed-off boss. But what many salespeople forget is that important activities should support impactful activities, not take the place of them. Your mission, then, is to train your AI tools to do these important things so that you remain focused on impactful things.

This requires ruthless prioritization. You need to get clear on exactly which activities you should be doing to make an impact and which ones you should not be doing, and when these things should be happening. Without this understanding, no investment in AI tools will give you more time to sell more.

Getting ruthless means you must say no to a lot of things you'll want to say yes to. Likewise, you may need to let go of some things you like to do, but AI can do better and faster, so that you may focus on your most impactful priorities. When you say yes to something trivial, for example, you are necessarily saying no to something that is important or impactful.

Ruthless prioritization is having the courage to say no to the small things so that you have time in your day for the big things. It means getting comfortable with standing up for yourself and disappointing others when you say no. It means getting stingy with your time. It requires discipline.

An easy way to prioritize is to break tasks into four categories:

- **Do:** Impactful things
- **Delete:** Trivial things
- **Delay:** Important things that only you can do
- **Delegate:** Important things that other people or AI should do

DELEGATE	DO
IMPORTANT THINGS THAT OTHERS OR AI SHOULD DO	IMPACTFUL THINGS THAT ONLY YOU ARE QUALIFIED TO DO
DELETE	DELAY
TRIVIAL THINGS THAT DISTRACT YOU FROM IMPORTANT AND IMPACTFUL THINGS	LOWER PRIORITY IMPACTFUL & IMPORTANT THINGS THAT ONLY YOU ARE QUALIFIED TO DO

Your daily mission is simple: squeeze as much out of the Golden Hours as possible by becoming disciplined with time.

Top sales pros fiercely protect the Golden Hours. They say no a lot. When a fellow rep stops by to chat them up about the weekend or bellyache about a recent policy change, they do not engage. When managers and corporate staff attempt to dump busy work on them, they push back. The best reps put "Do not disturb" signs on their doors to keep distractions at bay and leverage AI to do the things that take them away from impactful activities.

EXERCISE 12.1: PRIORITIZATION

Take a look at your current task list. Quickly write down your top five priorities ranked from highest priority to lowest. Then answer this question: Is this priority task moving me closer to my goals?

Priority	Is this priority moving you closer to your goals? Why or why not? What is the opportunity cost for focusing on this task?
1.	
2.	
3.	
4.	
5.	

EXERCISE 12.2: GET RUTHLESS

Next, put each task on your list into one of the four categories in the task prioritization matrix:

Delegate:	Do:
Delete:	Delay:

13

Attention Control and Time Blocking

L et's get real about the one thing AI cannot help you with: attention control. *The truth is that you are distracted. You are in a constant battle with your devices and the environment around you to maintain your attention and focus on the things that really matter.*

Disruptions and distractions barrage you from every direction: work, colleagues, home, personal life, email, chat, and that device in your pocket, stuck to you like glue, which dings, rings, and beeps all day long. It is a miracle that you can accomplish anything. Anthony has removed all social off his phone, along with notifications. You should do this too if you are tempted to stare into a screen instead of looking at a prospective client.

Efficiency decreases in direct proportion to the number of things you are attempting to do at one time. Recent research backs this up. Most sales professionals lose two to three hours a day of prime selling time to trivial distractions. Attention control is such a problem that the average time you spend on a task before getting distracted is around 11 minutes. Even worse, when you get distracted, it takes 25 minutes or more for you to recover your focus and get back on track.

The challenge is that your susceptibility to distractions is a human condition. Your brain is wired for distractions. It loves novel, bright, shiny things; this is called neomania—love of what is new.

Your brain gets bored quickly with repetitive tasks and seeks out stimulation. So, though AI can take many things off of your plate and never has a problem with attention control, it won't give you more time to sell more if you remain perpetually distracted. (Like any technology, AI itself could also pose a distraction in the future, so it's important to be able to manage your dependence on it.)

Intentional discipline to stay on task works for a while but is very difficult to sustain. Eventually your subconscious overrides your intentions and off you go chasing butterflies. Therefore, rather than fighting nature, you'll become far more productive if you organize your sales day to work with your brain rather than against it. The key to doing this is time blocking.

Time Blocking

Time blocking is a time management technique in which you segment your day into predefined blocks or chunks of time. Each block is dedicated to a specific task or focused activity. Instead of working in a reactive mode, responding to whatever comes up, you're proactively setting aside focused time for impactful and important priorities.

Time blocking is transformational for salespeople. It changes everything. When you get disciplined at blocking your time and concentrating your focus on only one thing at a time, you'll see a massive and profound impact on your productivity.

The key to becoming more effective in your sales day is frontloading your calendar with blocks of impactful activities that include prospecting, and synchronous conversations with prospects and customers. You should calendar three 90-minute blocks for impactful activities. That is 4.5 hours of your 8-hour working day. That leaves you with 3.5 hours for other activities. We advise you to make that first block prospecting.

You will become incredibly efficient once you realize that your brain was not made to talk, walk, rub your belly, and chew gum all at the same time. You simply cannot do multiple tasks simultaneously and do them well.

When you have too many things going on at once (especially complex tasks), your brain bogs down, and you slow down. It is no different from what happens when you have too many complex programs running at the same time on your computer. At some point the processor can't handle it and it runs slower and slower.

High-Intensity Activity Sprints

Parkinson's Law describes how work tends to expand to fill the time allotted for it. Give someone eight hours to do something that takes an hour—like make 30 prospecting calls—and it will take the entire eight hours. This is because your brain is distracted for the bulk of that time while it seeks out stimulation.

What your brain is exceptionally good at, though, is accomplishing a single task in short, high-intensity bursts. If you split that same activity into three 15-minute high-intensity sprints, you'll accomplish the task in 45 minutes or less.

When you block your day into short chunks of focused time for specific activities, you'll get more accomplished in a shorter time with far better results. You will be stunned at how productive you become when you leverage these high-intensity activity sprints and how you consistently get more done in less time than anyone on your team.

Building a solid foundation of time blocking, attention control, and time discipline matters because as you begin layering in AI tools, you'll experience an explosion in productivity that will translate to your sales performance and income.

14

Sales Day Planning, CRM, and Calendar Management

W*hat highly productive sales professionals have always done differently from their average and poor-performing peers is plan their week before the week begins. Average sellers typically start their morning with email and admin tasks, while poor performers jump into their day randomly with no plan at all. If this is you, stop it. You don't get paid for email or admin tasks.*

On the other hand, the highest earners don't wade into the day; they seize it. They work a plan that front-loads their day with impactful work that makes a difference and produces results. They ruthlessly prioritize and attack each sales day with intention.

The center of the universe for sales day planning is your calendar. Here you should have time blocked for impactful and important activities. You should be able to look at your calendar and know exactly what you need to do, where you need to be, whom you need to meet, and when those meetings will happen. Your calendar should also align with your daily task list and be connected to your email and CRM.

As we write this book there are dozens of new AI tools hitting the market to help with calendar planning and task management. Likewise Microsoft 365 and Google Workspaces (the two platforms used by most people in business) are integrating AI into their platforms to enhance and automate calendar and meeting management.

Promising Tools

The most promising AI tools connect your calendar, CRM, task list, and inbox together to help you prioritize people, prospects, and activities. Eventually AI will automate:

- High-priority prospecting lists
- Summaries of your upcoming day
- Task and communication prioritization
- Pre-call planning documents for each appointment
- Route mapping to make you more efficient in the field
- Calendar management

In the real world, though, not all of these new tools will be available to you. Most organizations won't allow you to indiscriminately download apps on your company-owned devices, nor will you have the personal budget to purchase multiple AI apps. Trust us, it gets expensive. Between us (Jeb and Anthony) we spend more than $2,000 per month on AI, and there is always another bright, shiny, new toy to experiment with.

With this in mind, the most important thing you can do is explore these new features and any new tools that you can access (based on your company's cybersecurity policy) and begin practicing. Not every tool will work for you but big changes are coming and you need to be ahead of the curve because calendar and task management is the one place where AI will have a massive and lasting impact on making you more efficient and effective.

The good news is that large companies, forward-thinking sales organizations, and cutting-edge executive leaders are all focused on finding ways to leverage AI in this area to give you more time to sell more. In the coming months and years these calendar, planning, territory mapping, and CRM management AI tools will be coming your way. It will be crucial for your income and career that you are prepared to become adept at using them.

AI Will Not Replace Human Intention

What AI will not replace is your intention and proven sales planning motions. AI may take the work out of gathering all of the information you need, but you must still put in the effort to get focused and build your roadmap to success.

Adopting a routine of weekly and daily calendar reviews leads to extraordinary performance improvement. Each Sunday evening or Monday morning before you begin your sales week:

- Invest an hour or so reviewing your calendar and each scheduled meeting with a prospect or customer for the upcoming week.
- Ensure that you have all of the materials organized for each meeting and consider your objective and desired outcomes for those sales conversations.
- Then set your goals for the week so that you have a roadmap for success.

Each evening before you leave work or go to bed:

- Review your achievements and accomplishments for the past day.
- Consider where you are relative to the goals you set for the week.
- Walk through each sales appointment for the next day to get mentally focused on winning in those sales conversations.
- Write down your three-highest-priority tasks or goals and resolve not to end the next day until those tasks are completed.

The good news is that AI will make sales day planning more efficient so that you can place your energy and focus on being more effective. Effective means starting your sales day knowing what must be done to accomplish your sales productivity goals with the mindset that nothing will stop you from making that happen.

Territory Mapping

The greatest waste of time for field sales pros is staring at a windshield. You start on one side of your territory to visit a prospect, then drive an hour in the other direction to another. You give no thought to that wasted hour because driving, moving, going to the next stop feels like work.

But it's not work. It's not selling. It's a delusion. Driving is not an accomplishment. Therefore, to be more productive, you must minimize drive time while maximizing human-to-human sales conversation time.

This is accomplished most effectively by mapping and segmenting your territory into small chunks—by Zip codes, counties, cities, or prospect and customer distribution—then breaking up your territory by day of the week (or month when working in large rural territories).

Once you have your territory mapped, group appointments and in-person prospecting activities inside of those segments and days. Be intentional about scheduling your day so that you avoid coloring outside of your daily territory segment lines.

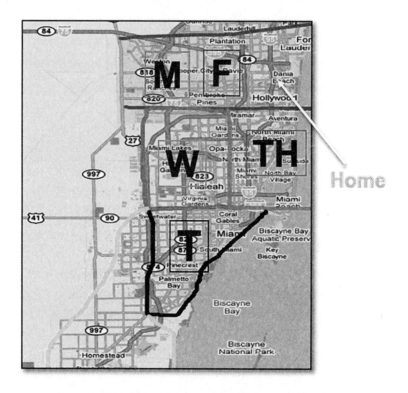

The good news is that AI is masterful at helping you with an understanding of where the opportunities in your territory are located. Modern mapping tools both inside and outside of your CRM greatly reduce the time it takes to develop a segmented territory map. These tools can also help you reduce wasted windshield time by building the most efficient route to each appointment.

The Hub-and-Spoke In-Person Prospecting System

The hub-and-spoke system for in-person prospecting will help you squeeze the most productivity out of your sales day. Using this system, you will plan five in-person prospecting calls in advance around your scheduled appointments.

This level of intention ensures that you are more likely to call on the most qualified opportunities in your territory, that you'll use the most efficient route to get to them, and that you'll be effective at engaging stakeholders and gatekeepers in conversations when you walk through their door.

The key to success is identifying prospective customers near your scheduled appointments and planning those prospecting touches in advance. AI mapping tools that connect with your CRM make this process much easier.

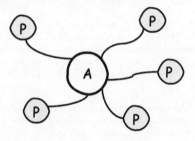

This process becomes even more effective when your AI prioritizes the prospects that you should be visiting, builds the route for you based on your territory plan and what is already on your calendar, and gives you a summary of what is already known about those prospects that prepares you to walk into those doors and engage them.

This is a future promise. For most salespeople, this high level of automation is years off. The good news is that AI can help you right now with in-person prospecting hub-and-spoke planning by scanning your prospects' websites and developing opening questions for you that will compel prospects to engage in conversations. Here's a simple example.

You

Review this website and give me three intriguing questions I can ask the owners: https://williamsseweranddrain.com/

ChatGPT

Based on the information gathered from Williams Sewer & Drain, Inc.'s website, here are three intriguing questions that you could ask the owners to engage them in a meaningful conversation:

1. **History and Evolution of Services**: "I noticed that Williams Sewer & Drain began as a septic tank pumping and cleaning company in 1969 and has since expanded its services significantly. Could you share more about this journey and how the company decided to diversify into areas like plumbing repairs, energy-efficient tankless water heaters, and portable restroom rentals?" This question relates to the company's history and growth, showing your interest in their long-term development and milestones [11] [11].

2. **Utilization of Advanced Technology**: "Your website mentions the use of state-of-the-art video technology for pinpointing exact locations of clogs or breaks in lines. How has this technology impacted your service efficiency and customer satisfaction?" This question highlights their adoption of advanced technology in their services, which is a point of pride and efficiency for many businesses [11].

3. **Team and Community Involvement**: "I read that Williams Sewer & Drain is a family-owned business with a strong team. Could you tell me more about how the team dynamics contribute to the success of your company? Also, are there any community events or initiatives that your company is particularly proud of being involved in?" This question focuses on the human aspect of their business and their community engagement, which can be a very engaging and personal topic for discussion [11].

These questions are designed to tap into the owners' pride in their business's history, technological advancements, team dynamics, and community involvement, which are often areas that business owners are eager and happy to discuss.

15

The First Seven Steps on Your AI Edge Journey

et's begin with a quick review of what we've learned so far: You get paid to sell. Robots get paid to give you more time to sell more. *But robots cannot choose how you invest your limited time, control your attention, or be intentional or disciplined for you. Only you can do that. Therefore, time discipline—sacrificing what you want now for what you want most—begins with the adoption of a CEO mindset and Me Management.*

Giving you more time for human-to-human conversations, problem-solving, and creativity is the primary purpose and priority for AI in sales. Because qualified pipeline opportunities are scarce and competition for the attention of buyers is fierce, the sales professionals who leverage AI to protect their prime selling time for human-centric activities will get ahead, stay ahead, and win while others lose.

Some sales reps will spend more time with their robots than with their prospective clients. They will harm their results, themselves, and their families.

Your mission then is to use AI in a manner that allows you to squeeze as much time out of your day for the things that *you* are uniquely qualified to do—your human advantage.

In modern selling there is a constant tension between goals and quotas and finding enough time to capture the opportunities that contribute to achieving those targets. The sheer pace of today's sales environment, with its endless flurry of internal emails, meetings, chats, CRM, and admin requirements, can often make us feel like we're caught in a relentless whirlwind in which we get nowhere. We find ourselves reacting, not strategizing. Busy, but not productive.

How, within this relentless storm of activities and demands, will you ever slow down long enough to harness AI in a positive and productive way? How can you gain the awareness and perspective to know where, when, and how to deploy AI in your sales day to give you more time to sell more?

Chinese philosopher Lao Tzo is credited with saying that a journey of a thousand miles begins with a single step. This oft-quoted adage highlights the importance of breaking overwhelming and daunting journeys into manageable parts. Your AI Edge journey begins with seven steps:

1. Conduct a Time Investment Audit to gain a clear understanding of what you are doing now.
2. Make a comprehensive list of the activities only you can do and which activities you should delegate to AI (or someone else).
3. Brainstorm all of the possibilities for how AI might put time back into your sales day.

4. Research and test AI tools and platforms.

5. Prioritize where and how you hand activities off to AI and integrate it into your sales process, planning, calendar management, and sales day.

6. Implement AI using the three A's: Adopt, Adapt, Adept.

7. Continue to repeat and refine this process until you've optimized your sales time for leveraging your human advantage.

The real secret to truly harnessing the power of AI is separating the things that only you can do from the things that robots can or should do. For example, only you can conduct synchronous, real-time, face-to-face conversations with other humans, whereas robots can and should do research, data crunching, and writing.

The only way to get to this separation, and a future state in which you have more time to sell, is to audit what you are actually doing now and get real about how you are currently investing your prime selling time. The next chapters dig more deeply into each of these steps.

16

Time Investment Audit

Wh…en we look at ultra-high performers in sales, a consistent pattern emerges. The highest earners have an acute awareness of how every minute of their day is utilized. Their superpower is clock mastering, not clock watching.

A Time Investment Audit helps put into sharp focus how you are actually using time. It's a transformative lens. Through it, you'll be able to quickly identify the activities that drive sales from those that drain your time, energy, joy, and income.

In today's interconnected world, disruptions are the norm. When it comes to ruthless prioritization, the devil's in the details. Those "quick" admin tasks or "short" unscheduled calls? They add up, stealthily eating into your prime selling hours. But through an audit, we can recognize them, address them, and shield our prime selling hours.

Conducting an audit of how you spend your Golden Hours is invaluable for improving your productivity and effectiveness.

It will help you gain clarity for how AI can truly help you. The audit helps you elevate and break down your daily routine— moment to moment and hour to hour. It creates awareness, which is a prerequisite for change.

Define Your Prime Selling Time

Before you assess how you're using your prime selling time, start by clearly defining what constitutes this period for you. These Golden Hours are typically the window during the day when your prospects and customers are most receptive to discussions and when you're most energized and focused. For most sellers this will be 8 a.m. to 5 p.m., but it may be different for you depending on your industry.

Data Collection and Activity Log

For at least one week (preferably two), keep a detailed log of your activities. Break each day into 15-minute or 30-minute blocks and jot down what you're doing in each slot. Classify each activity into categories, including:

- Distractions and interruptions
- Prospecting
- Social media business
- Social media personal
- Customer meetings and interactions
- Team meetings, company meetings, one-to-ones
- Following up and advancing pipeline opportunities
- Administrative tasks and getting stuff done time
- Travel and windshield time
- Breaks and personal time
- Training and professional development

- Family and fun time
- Any other tasks specific to your role

EXERCISE 16.1: ACTIVITY LOG

Time	Activities	Impactful, Important, or Trivial
7:00 AM		
7:30 AM		
8:00 AM		
8:30 AM		
9:00 AM		
9:30 AM		
10:00 AM		
10:30 AM		
11:00 AM		
11:30 AM		
12:00 PM		
12:30 PM		
1:00 PM		
1:30 PM		
2:00 PM		
2:30 PM		
3:00 PM		
3:30 PM		
4:00 PM		
4:30 PM		
5:00 PM		
5:30 PM		

Data Analysis

Calculate the percentage of time spent on each activity category during your prime selling hours. Then identify impactful activities that directly contribute to revenue generation, important activities that support revenue generation, and trivial activities that distract you from impactful activities.

When possible, research how the highest-performing salespeople in your company are spending their prime selling time and use that as a benchmark. Then answer these questions:

- Is how you are investing your time moving you closer or taking you farther away from achieving your sales and income goals?
- Which activities are dominating your golden hours?
- Which tasks can be delegated, automated, or eliminated?
- What disruptions or distractions keep reoccurring?
- How do you deal with distractions?
- Which activities and tasks are wasting your time and adding no value to your sales day?
- Which specific behavior patterns are eroding your productivity?

Look in the mirror. Get honest with yourself. Seek feedback from your manager and peers. Keep asking questions until you have a clear view of your time investment gaps.

Set New Goals

By following this structured approach, you'll get a clear view of how you're spending your prime selling time and awareness of how to make the best use of it. Remember, the goal isn't just about being busy; it's about being productive and effective in generating sales.

We all know that we should eat better, exercise more, and get enough sleep. We know it, but we don't do it because doing it is hard. Once you have analyzed how you are actually using your time you have a choice to make. You can *know* it or you can *do* something about it.

Doing something about it means making conscious, intentional decisions about reallocating your time. It means prioritizing revenue-generating tasks during your prime selling hours. If there are important, nonpriority tasks that need to be done daily, consider how they might be automated or scheduled outside of your prime selling time.

To-Do List and To-Don't List

You'll likely need to make changes to how you start your day, end your day, and block activities on your calendar in between. You'll need a *to-do* list and a *to-don't* list.

A list of things you are not willing to do will help you better manage your time. What would go on a to-don't list?

- *Don't open email first thing in the morning.* Your inbox is a place where other people send you their to-do list. Until you complete your first impactful block of the day, don't open your inbox. People will call you if they have a serious issue that needs your attention.

- *Don't allow people to interrupt your focus blocks.* This means setting clear boundaries to minimize disruptions. This might involve setting specific times for checking emails or using "Do Not Disturb" modes to keep interruptions out of your environment.

- *Don't let other people place their priorities above yours.* You can make exceptions when it makes sense.

The Time Investment Audit is more than a mechanism; it's a manifesto. A commitment to valuing every second, to channeling every minute toward sales success, getting disciplined with time, sacrificing what you want now for what you want most.

The journey to mastering sales begins with mastering time. With the Time Investment Audit as your compass, the path to sales excellence becomes clear and compelling. Now, with a clearer picture of how you are actually spending your time, identifying where and how AI can and should help you get more time to sell more becomes more targeted and infinitely easier.

17

Brainstorming and Prioritizing AI Possibilities

Now that you're thinking about how you spend your time, let's brainstorm a list of the work, activities, and tasks that you'd like to give to AI. As a refresher, brainstorming is a problem-solving technique that involves throwing spontaneous ideas on the wall without judging them. You can do it yourself, but it is even more fun and effective to do with a team. Here are some ideas to get you started:

Outreach

- **Email management:** For most salespeople, email takes a big bite out of the day. So, it's no surprise that time management and email management go hand in hand.

Artificial intelligence can help you write, organize, and prioritize your emails automatically, so you can spend less time in your inbox.

- **Scheduling send times:** Optimize email send times by analyzing when each recipient is most likely to engage. Then you can draft emails when that activity best fits into your day without having to sync up your schedule with the recipient.

- **Content sharing:** AI can suggest and create posts for sharing on LinkedIn or other platforms to help you maintain an active presence without having to dedicate so much time to research and early drafts. Remember, though, that AI is a tool, so you can't accept what it puts in front of you as truth. You still need to check everything and put your own spin on things, but AI can reduce the amount of time you spend staring at your screen hoping an idea for a post comes to you.

- **Media:** Create engaging media using AI to generate relevant text and data visualizations.

- **Engagement optimization:** AI can identify optimal times and contexts to engage with prospects' posts or messages.

Daily Tasks

- **Research automation:** AI can research far faster than you can. This doesn't mean you don't need to do the reading and the work, but it can wrangle useful sources so you don't have to spend time looking for them. Before a meeting, AI can scour the web and pull everything together for you, so you have a nice stack of digital resources to read as you prepare for sales conversations.

- **Agenda setting:** AI can suggest agendas and talking points based on prior interactions and customer profiles, stakeholder personas, and individual communication styles (for example, DISC or Jeb's A.C.E.D. style types[1]).
- **Automated CRM data entry:** AIs can enter relevant email and call data into your CRM to minimize manual entry, along with information it collects from other online sources. This works much the same way that AI can populate your calendar based on meeting invitations and email content.
- **Alerts for follow-ups:** AI can automate reminders for follow-ups based on prior interactions with prospects and customers.
- **Quick edits:** AI can suggest quick improvements and edits in your documents, ensuring they are error-free and polished.

Me Management
- **Task prioritization:** Utilize AI to prioritize daily tasks based on urgency and importance.
- **Sales day optimization:** AI can suggest the best times to make calls, arrange meetings, or engage in prospecting activities.
- **Time tracking:** AI-powered time-tracking tools help you gain insight into where your time is going, all without having to deal with a manual timer.
- **Automated scheduling:** AI can manage scheduling workflow to simplify the scheduling process, using algorithms to arrange the day for you.

---

[1]Learn more about communicating with A.C.E.D. stakeholder-style types in Jeb's book *Sales EQ: How Ultra-High Performers Leverage Sales-Specific Emotional Intelligence to Close the Complex Deal* (Wiley, 2017).

- **Prioritization of tasks:** AI can analyze task lists in real time, prioritizing items based on their due dates, statuses, and more. AI-powered prioritization helps you manage tasks and tackle work in the most effective way possible, so you can make the most of your time and energy.

- **Personalized reminders:** Like a great assistant, AI can offer personalized reminders that help you stay on track. You can tailor these notifications according to your preferences and get them delivered through various channels, like email, Google Chat, MS Teams, or Slack.

Prospecting

- **Opportunity finder:** Use AI to identify networking opportunities and events where prospects might be present.

- **Intent and buying windows:** Identifying which prospects are more likely to buy or are moving into a buying window.

- **List building:** AI can analyze mountains of intent data, combined with ideal qualifying checkpoints to build high-probability prospecting lists.

- **Connection suggestions:** AI can recommend new social media connections based on mutual interests, common connections, or potential business synergies.

Strategic Thinking

- **Brainstorming:** AI can help you with brainstorming ideas by adding to what you are able to generate on your own (a very cool use of generative AI).

- **Pre-call planning:** When you are getting ready for sales conversations, AI can help with finding information on stakeholders and companies, scanning through and summarizing documents, pointing to where there may be pain or opportunities to solve problems, and developing discovery questions.
- **Deal prediction:** Using historical data, AI can predict which deals are most likely to close, which helps you prioritize and invest your time on pipeline opportunities with the highest win probability.
- **Risk alerts:** AI can send alerts for deals that may be at risk, helping you increase or change communication when it's most needed and allowing for timely intervention.
- **Account expansion and retention:** For account managers and customer success professionals AI can identify opportunities for upsells and cross-selling. It can also identify which customers are most at risk and help improve net revenue retention.
- **Competitor analysis:** AI can provide insights into competitors' strategies and offerings, helping a salesperson stay informed and prepare rebuttals to competitor claims.

Professional Development

- **Sales performance tracking:** Keeping track of personal sales metrics and KPIs to continuously evaluate and improve performance requires a great deal of human energy. AI can surface this data much faster and more accurately.
- **Improvement recommendations:** AI can crunch your sales numbers and provide suggestions for areas of improvement based on performance analytics.

- **Continuous learning:** Based on what you want to learn or may be interested in, AI can recommend articles, videos, and courses to help you stay abreast of industry trends and enhance your skills.

Prioritize Return on Investment

The universe of AI-powered tools is exploding. There are myriad applications on the market right now that can make your life significantly more efficient. Many more are on the horizon.

Some of these applications will be integrated into the tools you already use, such as your calendar, CRM, and email platform. Others will need to be purchased separately and may not be available to you depending on your company's policies.

What you can count on, though, is that if you are paying for tools out of your own pocket, you'll need to be prepared for sticker shock. AI is expensive. Therefore, as you prioritize what you plan to give to AI, be sure you'll get a reasonable return on your investment and that the price you pay is worth the time you could gain.

AI Adoption Is a Marathon, Not a Sprint

When used effectively, AI will allow you to laser-focus on the things that you do best and that make you happy. It will not only put hours back into your sales day and personal life, but it will take away activities that steal your joy. This is one of the great promises of AI.

It won't solve all of your problems, nor will you be able to unload everything you dislike, but when you consider all that you do as a sales professional, the possibilities for leveraging AI are mind-boggling. However, gaining an AI Edge in sales will be a long and winding journey, a marathon rather than a sprint.

Let's begin your journey with four exercises to spark your imagination about what is possible and help you prioritize what you should give to AI and what you should keep. As you approach these exercises, answer these questions about the activities and tasks that take up your time:

- Is this something that is aligned with your purpose?
- Is spending time on a task something that provides meaning in your life?
- Does the activity move you closer to your goals?
- Do you enjoy this work?
- If you don't enjoy the work, is it impactful and mission-critical work that you must and should do?
- Is this work that only you can do?
- Do you bring special value to the work that no machine can do nearly as well as you?
- Does this work make a unique and impactful contribution to your company, income, customers, family, or life?
- Can you give yourself over to the activity and do your very best work?
- How much time do you spend on this work now and why?
- How much time are you spending now on activities that give you joy and only you can do?
- How much time are you spending on activities that steal your joy that AI can do better than you?

EXERCISE 17.1: ENJOYABLE SALES ACTIVITIES

Brainstorm and make a list of the sales activities that you most enjoy in your role as a sales professional or sales leader and why you enjoy these activities.

Sales Activities You Enjoy	Why?

Take a good look at this list. It should be filled with the things that you, as a human, are uniquely equipped to do and do well.

When you consider which activities you should hand over to your robot, use this list as a guide. Certainly, there may be some things on this list that AI can do for you, but that doesn't mean that you should hand them over to a bot. Remember Robot Rule three: Just because AI can, doesn't mean it should. Never allow AI to steal your joy!

Keeping it real, there may not be an AI solution at the moment, for every activity. However, those solutions are likely right around the corner, so you'll want to keep your eyes and ears open as the technology advances.

EXERCISE 17.2: ACTIVITIES THAT IMPEDE SELLING

Next, make a list of the tasks and activities that you feel hold you back from prospecting, engaging stakeholders in synchronous conversations, deal strategy, creative problem-solving, and advancing opportunities through your pipeline (and other impactful sales activities). Describe why these activities have this negative effect.

Activities That Impede Selling	Why?

As you review this list, consider which of these activities you'd gladly hand over to your robot if you could teach it how to do the activity. This will inform your search for AI tools, techniques, systems, and processes for taking these things off of your plate.

EXERCISE 17.3: KEEP OR GIVE AWAY

Finally, make a short-term *priority* list of the sales and Time Management Activities that you will keep and those that you will give away to your robot, based on the technology that is available today. This is where you should begin your AI journey.

Sales Time Management Activities You Will Keep	Sales Time Management Activities You Will Give Away

If what you are doing doesn't move you closer to your goals, isn't meaningful, or doesn't bring you joy, you need to find a way to avoid that work. Delegate it. Defer it. Delete it. Automate it with AI. Remember, you aren't going to have any more time. This is it, baby, so make it count!

EXERCISE 17.4: IDENTIFY AI TOOLS FOR YOUR PRIORITIES

Finally, make a short-term *priority* list of the sales and time management activities that you will keep and those that you will give away to your robot, based on the technology that is available today. This is where you should begin your AI journey.

Sales and Time Management Activities to Prioritize for AI Delegation	Preferred AI Tool, Platform, Software, Widget

18

Practice and Prompts

M*alcolm Gladwell popularized the 10,000-hour rule in his book* Outliers. *The concept he touted is that it takes 10,000 hours of deliberate practice to master any discipline.*

What few people know is that the person who originally developed the 10,000-hour rule was K. Anders Ericsson, a Swedish psychologist and professor of psychology at Florida State University. His theory was based on his observations of the practicing habits of the great masters of chess, music, sports, and medicine.

Though there is debate about whether 10,000 hours is a magic number, there is little disagreement that deliberate, dedicated time invested in practice will improve your competency in most disciplines.[1] Sadly, most people fail to ever reach a level of competence with things they attempt to master because getting good at anything is frustratingly hard. Because practice isn't fun, most people give up too soon.

---

[1] https://www.bbc.com/future/article/20121114-gladwells-10000-hour-rule-myth

It is no different with AI. It's hard. Practicing with different AI prompts can be maddening, like attempting to figure out a puzzle blindfolded while riding a horse that is on fire.

Learning how to use AI effectively is frustrating, just as it is when you attempt to learn anything new. There will be times when it feels like it's taking longer to delegate the task to the robot than to just do it yourself.

You'll want to give up. Don't. No one gets it completely right instantly. Give it time. Strive for progress rather than perfection. Avoid reverting to old habits. The more you practice, the more

EXERCISE 18.1: AI TOOL INVENTORY

Make a list of the AI applications you are already using and rate your competency with each tool from 1 to 5, with 5 being an expert power user, and 1 being a beginner. Then resolve to practice to raise your competency with each tool using prompt engineering, which we cover next.

AI Application	How/Why/When You Use It	Competency Level (1–5)

progress you'll make, until what was once a struggle is now effortless second nature.

To become adept with new tools, you must slow down and practice in order to speed up. The key is the deliberate, intentional practice that Ericsson championed. This means setting aside time that will be specifically invested in learning and mastering AI. This practice must be ongoing because AI will continue to evolve and change.

Prompt Engineering

Prompt engineering is the process of structuring text into a format that can be interpreted and understood by generative AI.

AI tools are trained on massive datasets of text and code. They can generate text, translate languages, write different kinds of creative sales content, and answer your questions in an informative way. But only if you know how to ask the right questions, in the right format.

A prompt is a natural language text that describes the task that an AI should perform. Essentially, prompts are how we speak to AI using its language.

For example, the prompt "Write a poem about a cat" tells your robot to generate a poem about a cat. But you might not like what you get with such a general and broad request. Therefore, to get what you want you'll need to include additional information, such as the style of the poem, the context for the poem, or the desired length. You might instead prompt, "Write a poem about a cat, walking through the woods, on a moonless night, in the style of Edgar Allan Poe."

Just for fun, here is what AI produced:

In the shadowed woods, where whispers dwell, A velvet paw, a silent bell. Through the dark, where sight does fail, Wanders the cat, with coat so pale.

No moon to cast her silver light, No stars to crown the ebon night. Yet onward moves the feline grace, Each step a ghost, without a trace.

The trees, like specters, tall and grim, Stand watchful as she threads through them. Their branches stir, a creaking moan, In forests deep, where light has flown.

What secrets does she seek to find, Within this night, so dark, so blind? An owl's hoot, a rustle low, The woods alive with tales of woe.

Yet fear, a stranger to her heart, For she in darkness plays her part. With eyes that gleam like amber fire, She roams the woods, ne'er to tire.

Beneath the canopy of gloom, Where shadows dance and fancies loom, She finds her path, her silent quest, In Poe's own words, a soul at rest.

The goal of prompt engineering is to write prompts that are clear, concise, and produce the information you seek on the first try. You need to know what you want at the outset and design your prompt around it, instead of plugging in less specific prompts and hoping AI lands on something close. The prompt should be specific enough to tell the AI tool what to do, but it should not be so specific that it limits creativity. The prompt should also be grammatically correct and free of errors.

Here are some basic examples of prompt engineering:

- Translate this sentence from English to French.
- Answer the following question: What is the capital of France?

- Generate a code snippet that prints "Hello, world!" to the console.
- Write a creative story about a robot who falls in love with a human.

Effective prompt engineering is crucial because the way a question or prompt is phrased can significantly impact output and the usefulness of the response. Another way of looking at it is that the fewer times you have to prompt the AI tool, the faster you get what you need, and the more time you gain to sell more.

Practice Building a Prompt

As you get started with prompts, you may have to try a number of configurations before you land on one that does exactly what you want. Building prompts is a skill that has an inherent level of fluidity.

There is no common prompt engineering manual, because even the geniuses who build and train AI don't know exactly how to create a failsafe recipe. And since AI is always learning and evolving, its capabilities are always growing. Therefore, the prompts that you use today may give you a different result in the future, or even the next time you use them.

For example, Anthony spent hours developing a complex prompt that worked for months and then suddenly stopped working. He ended up asking his AI to rebuild the prompt to make it work again.

The good news is that if a prompt isn't returning what you need, you can always ask your AI to help you build a prompt. The first time I tried to build a complex prompt, it didn't work. I wanted to automate adding the hyperlinks to my blog posts, which would save a ton of time. I tried every combination of words I could think of but nothing worked.

Then I had a crazy idea. Who knows better than the AI itself? So I typed, "Can you help me build a prompt that will add the hyperlinks in a blog post?" I watched in awe as the AI built the prompt for me. It worked perfectly.

Senator and businessman Chauncey Depew said that the first step toward getting somewhere is to decide that you are not going to stay where you are. Accordingly, the path to mastering AI prompts to make you faster, better, and stronger is the decision to jump in and get started. That's exactly what we're going to do over the next set of exercises.

EXERCISE 18.2: GET FAMILIAR WITH GENERATIVE AI PROMPTS

Go to your browser and open ChatGPT (https://chat.openai .com/) in one tab, Google Gemini in the next tab (https:// gemini.google.com/app), and Claude (https://claude.ai/ chats) in another.

Start with this prompt: "List the top 50 books of literature ranked by page count."

Observe the differences between the three platforms and the quality of the outputs. This should help you get a feel for what to expect with a broad, subjective prompt and how AIs that have been trained on different data sets perform.

The lesson is that as AI platforms proliferate, we'll need to hone our prompts for each one.

Next try Jeb's favorite prompt: List the winningest Georgia Bulldog football teams by year and win-loss record in table format.

Notice the quality of the output and how including "in table format" organized the data. Still, the three platforms produced different results, which is why it pays to practice and try prompts on different platforms.

Pro Tip: What's brilliant about Google Gemini is that it makes it easy to export your output directly into Google Sheets, saving you even more time.

Go Dawgs!

EXERCISE 18.3: PRACTICE A SALES PROMPT

Let's dive in and practice a sales specific prompt. Try both prompts below and observe the output:

- **ChatGPT:** "List the top five competitors of https:// williamsseweranddrain.com/, including websites, phone numbers, and the name of the CEO or owner in table format."
- **Google Gemini:** "List the top five competitors of Williams Sewage and Drain that are located in Augusta, GA."

Consider how you might use this prompt in your territory for prospecting.

EXERCISE 18.4: WRITE YOUR OWN PROMPTS

It's time to stretch your AI prompt engineering prowess as you build your own prompts.

- **Prompt One:** Choose a targeted prospect. Write a prompt that will cause your AI to teach you about their industry and the challenges they may face in their business.

- **Prompt Two:** Write a prompt that will cause your AI to describe your prospect's value proposition and how it helps customers.

Take time to reconfigure and refine your prompts until you get exactly what you are looking for. Then add those new prompts to your prompt library.

Build a Sales Prompt Library

What you want to avoid doing is reinventing the wheel each time you need something from AI. That will cost you a lot of time. Instead, when you find a prompt that works for you, add it to your prompt library to make it easy to reference when you need it in the future.

For example, Anthony's prompt library includes the following prompts:

- *Crit* that criticizes his writing
- *English* that provides him with a table of problems in written communications he prepares for clients
- *Tweet* that turns his blog articles into a set of social media posts

This table contains some examples to get you started with your own prompt library.

Prompt Name	Platform	Purpose	Prompt	Notes
Editor	ChatGPT	Edit your writing without allowing GPT to rewrite your text.	*You are a world-class English editor. Edit the following article without rewriting the original, unless you need to correct a misspelling, add a missing word, or fix a grammar problem or a syntax error. When you are done, make a table of the edits you made.*	The table will let you check the AI's edits. On occasion, GPT rewrites your text. If that happens, tell it to start over.
Criticism	ChatGPT	Improve your writing with specific suggestions.	*Please analyze [your subject/ work] and identify areas where improvements can be made. Offer specific suggestions and recommendations on how to enhance these aspects in order to achieve better results or performance.*	You will need to decide what will improve your text and what won't make the text better.

(Continued)

Prompt Name	Platform	Purpose	Prompt	Notes
LinkedIn Post	ChatGPT	Turn a piece of text into a LinkedIn post.	*Please turn this article into a LinkedIn Post with [eight] bullet points and emojis and focus on [Topic]. Please don't use the words "LinkedIn Fam," and write in second person.*	If your company posts blog posts or other content, this prompt will turn it into a LinkedIn Post with emojis.
Insights on Industry Trends	Gemini	Research and understand a certain industry.	*You are a world-class researcher on [industry] and provide me with a list of the headwinds and tailwinds this industry is experiencing with data points on each trend.*	ChatGPT doesn't always do the best work on this prompt. Bard seems to do a better job because it is connected to the internet.
Insight Prospecting Email for a Leader	ChatGPT	Write an email with insights and data about the industry's challenges and a strong call to action.	*You are a world-class copywriter. You are also a world-class expert in the oil and gas industry. Write a short sales prospecting email with two insights about the industry with a strong call to action.*	You will need to edit this work before sending it to anyone.

Prompt Name	Platform	Purpose	Prompt	Notes
Assess risks in a client's contract	Claude.ai or ChatGPT	Identify the risks you may be taking on by signing your client's contract.	*You are a world-class contract lawyer who is conservative about signing contracts. What risks should I be concerned about and why?*	Don't worry that the AI will say you need a lawyer. Claude.ai can process 400 pages in about three minutes.
Edit the contract clause to make it less of a risk	Claude.ai or ChatGPT	You can reduce the risk by having AI rewrite the contract.	*You are a world-class contract lawyer who has been retained to rewrite this clause to make it fair to both parties or reciprocal.*	This works well for indemnification and other legal commitments that might be a problem and unfair.
Diplomatic Tone	ChatGPT	Have AI make sure your text doesn't offend your client.	*Edit this text to ensure that nothing written will cause offense.*	You know how sometimes what you write is read in a way that offends the person receiving it? This will ensure you don't offend. You may need to edit the text, but AI is more objective than you might be.

(Continued)

Prompt Name	Platform	Purpose	Prompt	Notes
Summarize and Prepare for Sales Meetings	ChatGPT	Summarize my last interactions.	*Please summarize the attached notes and summarize each interaction by date and highlight any commitments I owe this client.*	If you use a recording AI, this will be really helpful. But because you can use a PDF of your notes, it will still help you prepare for a meeting.
Characteristics of Decision Makers	ChatGPT	Understand leaders' psychographics and the behaviors of decision makers	*Provide me with the psychographic and behavioral characteristics of senior leaders of [industry], like [company], [company], and [company].*	This prompt will help you prepare for a meeting with a contact by helping you know how they think and behave.
Best Approach	ChatGPT	Determine how best to approach a leader with a new opportunity to improve an important outcome.	*How should I approach these leaders with an opportunity to improve [outcome]?*	This prompt will help you with prospecting messaging.

EXERCISE 18.5: SET UP YOUR PROMPT LIBRARY

Take a moment now to set up your prompt engineering library. Start with the prompts in the table in this chapter and build your own as you become more skilled. If you are already using certain prompts, add them to your library. Then as you discover new prompts that work, build your library with them.

Throughout this book, you'll find more proven prompts to add to your prompt engineering library. Your best bet is to store this on a document or spreadsheet in the cloud so that it is easy to access. Then, whenever you need a prompt, you can copy it from your library right into the tool of your choice. There are also applications like *Magical* that will store your prompt library and allow you to build shortcuts to automate AI prompt entry, saving you even more time.

Stick with It

In Part 4 we dive into the one area where AI has the greatest potential to make you better and more efficient: *writing and communicating*. This is where the right prompts used in the right context can save you hundreds of hours per year and improve the quality of your written communication tenfold.

Helen Keller said that we can do anything we want if we stick with it long enough. Keep working on your prompts. To gain the competitive edge you seek, you must remain on the leading edge of technology and this requires curiosity, exploration, and lots of practice.

PART 4

Writing, Grammar, and Communication

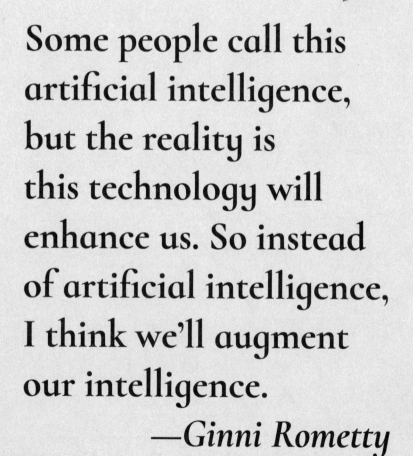

Some people call this artificial intelligence, but the reality is this technology will enhance us. So instead of artificial intelligence, I think we'll augment our intelligence.

—*Ginni Rometty*

19

If It Quacks Like a Duck

At dinner, a good friend of mine, the CEO of a fast-growing tech company, read out loud the article his public relations vendor sent him to approve. As he worked his way through it, he muttered, "That's got to change. That's not going to work. We need a different phrase for that."

As I listened, the patterns sounded very familiar. When he finished, I said matter-of-factly, "That piece was written entirely by a robot. My guess is ChatGPT."

He shook his head, "That can't be. I pay them way too much to do something like that!"

"Well, they spent all of about five minutes on the article," I responded. "You need to get your money back!"

Still in disbelief, he sent a text message to his account manager at the PR firm and asked about it. She confirmed that, yes, they had used ChatGPT to write the piece about him and his company. It was a cringeworthy moment, and the pained look of betrayal on his face made me regret having said anything.

In an instant, he had lost trust in his vendor. Their value, in his eyes, had diminished significantly. It was the beginning of the end of that relationship, and the loss of tens of thousands of dollars in fees for the PR firm.

Humans Resent Being Manipulated

Let us accept that this PR firm's intent was noble—that they wanted to create an engaging article for their client. Yet, they made two grave mistakes.

First, they made my friend feel that he had been manipulated, as most people do once they realize that they are dealing with a robot under false pretenses. This is exactly why the number-one question we get on inbound chat conversations on our websites is "Are you a robot?" People want to know up front whether they are talking to a human or AI so that they can adjust their expectations.

Second, the PR firm devalued their brand and lost my friend's respect by putting zero effort into a project that was very important to him. He also felt cheated because he had paid for their expertise, but they didn't bother using it. What they sent to him was something he could have had ChatGPT write on his own.

This is important, so pay attention. Humans have little respect for people who take shortcuts and don't put in the effort. It makes us feel like they don't care. This is why setting-it-and-forgetting-it with generative AI is a wickedly stupid strategy that will eventually destroy your relationships with other humans.

People Don't Trust Robots

There are always people who want to cheat nature. The problem with trying to cheat nature is that nature has been around a lot longer than you and I have, and it cheats back.

These days, sales reps are sending prospects a massive amount of email that is clearly written by robots. AI's patterns stand out and are so easy to spot that it takes mere seconds to mark these messages as spam and block the senders. This is exactly why the major email service providers have put into place rules to end this practice. This disingenuous approach does not work and has quickly led to the demise and devaluation of prospecting email.

Prospects and customers everywhere are taking notice. People are not stupid. They can tell when you are making little effort and taking shortcuts. They are intuitive enough to see robot patterns. When you look like a robot, act like a robot, and write like a robot, then, to them, you are a robot. And the brutal truth is that humans don't trust robots.[1]

The human advantage is authenticity, empathy, creativity, randomness, fallibility, and unpredictability. It is demonstrating that you care and value your prospects and customers by putting in real effort to win their business. To get ahead and stay ahead in an AI-dominated world, you must learn to lean into those things that make you uniquely human.

AI Can Never Be You

There are so many ways AI fails to be human, but none of them mean that you should avoid it altogether. Instead, you should plug into AI to help you move faster and smarter. AI can and will do incredible things for you, including writing

---

[1] Zhang, G., et al. "Trust in an AI versus a Human teammate: The effects of teammate identity and performance on Human-AI cooperation," *Computers in Human Behavior* 139, February 2023. Available at: https://doi.org/10.1016/j.chb.2022.107536.

articles, emails, meeting summaries, social media posts, proposals, scripts, and anything else you feed it. But don't abandon your human abilities by handing everything over to AI without deep consideration for the unintended consequences.

AI cannot be *you*. Therefore, you should never, ever, ever set it and forget it. You must take the time to humanize anything the AI produces for you—even after using prompts that encourage AI to do this for you.

Just imagine the different outcome had my friend's PR firm used the AI-generated article as a foundation and then put in the effort to edit and rewrite it to remove the robot patterns and give it a real, authentic human tone. They could have made sure the final version reflected my friend's values, which they knew based on their conversations. That type of insight is something AI has difficulty capturing, even if humans try to feed it into their prompts.

While generative AI can process information and generate text at superhuman speeds and volumes, it lacks genuine understanding or emotional context. As we continue to integrate AI into our daily lives, maintaining a clear distinction between machine-generated content and human interaction will be of paramount importance.

Most significantly, especially when you are using AI for messaging and writing, pay close attention to the feedback from your prospects and customers, whether it's good, bad, or ugly. If your messages are being deleted without being read, reconsider what you are saying and how you are communicating. Use this feedback to hone your approach, your prompts, and your own edits so that your messages feel and sound authentically human.

Here is a list of words humans rarely use that can cause the reader to recognize it was written by a robot:

- Akin
- Delve
- Facilitate
- Subsequently
- Encompass
- Alleviate
- Comprise
- Embark
- Foremost
- Pertinent
- Advocate for
- In light of
- Invariably
- Intricacies
- Paramount
- Mitigate
- Augment
- Intrinsically
- Synergize
- Viable
- Analogous
- Catalyst
- Expound
- Utilize
- Efficacious
- Notwithstanding
- Profound
- Foster
- Preeminent
- Expedite

AI as Your Writing Partner

Let's quickly review. When AI is used incorrectly with indiscriminate copying and pasting, it can and will damage relationships and make you look incompetent and lazy. By contrast, when you use it intentionally, combined with your human advantage, it will save you a massive amount of time and make your written communications infinitely better.

The ways that AI can help with writing are so plentiful and at times complex that including them all is beyond the scope of this book. So instead of fire-hosing you with every possible use case and prompt, let's focus on the most frequent and fundamental ways to leverage it to improve and speed up your written communication:

- Editing
- Spell-checking
- Summarizing and creating bullet points
- Grammar checking
- Word replacement and thesaurus
- Finding missing words
- Tone and style changes
- Shortening sentences
- Tightening up long documents
- Honing vocabulary
- Writing from scratch
- Writing in your voice
- Writing in another voice
- Writing in another language

To get the most out of AI as a writing tool, start by getting better at the fundamentals of writing, including sentence structure, grammar, and editing. Once you understand these foundational rules, you can begin to truly unlock the power of AI for written communication. It is very, very powerful.

20

Write and Edit Better

O*kay, we're just going to step up and say it, but don't kill the messengers. Most salespeople wouldn't know good grammar and sentence structure if it walked up to them wearing a unicorn costume and hit them in the face with a two-by-four.*

Sales professionals are good at talking, presenting, sketching pictures on whiteboards, and getting people to say yes to all kinds of things. But writing, nope. Not a strong point.

Still, writing matters to making a good impression, as much as how you dress, speak, and present yourself. When your written communication is poor, people judge you for it. You are perceived as uneducated, untrustworthy, lazy, uncaring, and unprofessional—all things that can kill you in highly competitive situations where deals are often won or lost by an edge.

Writing is power. Effective writing gives you the ability to:

- Communicate effectively in written format, allowing you to extend your influence beyond the stakeholders you know to those you don't.

- Sell your ideas and solutions when you are not physically there, especially as the complexity increases, the buying committee grows, and the sales cycle lengthens.
- Advance your career and get promotions and raises.
- Build your personal brand and demonstrate your expertise, knowledge, and thought leadership.
- Negotiate for what you want more effectively.

Get Better at the Craft of Business Writing Without AI

Just as you learned with time management in the previous section, you need a good foundation in the fundamentals of writing and grammar before you leverage AI effectively to make yourself better. To do this you'll need to put in the effort to study and practice structuring sentences, building vocabulary, and learning basic grammar.

It is true that our modern education system has failed many young professionals by not teaching them how to write effectively. But this is not an excuse! Please stop with the "I can't write" bullshit story that you keep telling yourself and others. As long as you keep saying what you can't do, that's exactly what you'll get.

You can learn to write better if you make that choice. We know this firsthand as authors because when we first started out, our writing was terrible—embarrassingly bad. (This is especially true if you grew up on a back-country dirt road in Georgia, like one of us.)

Over time, though, our writing improved. What changed was practice, study, learning from criticism, working with editors, reading, and doing it. Lots and lots of doing it.

Remember the 10,000-hour rule? It turns out that the more you write, the better you get at writing. Even though we sucked at writing when we started (and still do from time to time), we've leveraged the written word to build successful global businesses and make an impact on millions of people. Today, people all over the world read our books and articles.

We cannot emphasize enough how crucial it is to get better at writing without AI before you start using AI to make you even better. Start now by reading *On Writing Well* by Brian Zinsser. This book will make you better (almost instantly), guaranteed. We also recommend the *HBR Guide to Better Business Writing*. Buy these books and read them!

We also recommend investing in Grammarly. Grammarly is a writing assistance tool that uses artificial intelligence and natural language processing to help improve written communication. It checks for various types of errors, including grammar, punctuation, spelling, and style. Then it offers suggestions to make the text clearer, more concise, and more effective.

The key to improving writing skills is paying attention to the explanations Grammarly gives for its corrections, which can help you learn from mistakes and improve your writing skills over time. Regular use surfaces common mistakes and weaknesses in your writing. This ongoing feedback loop leads to a better understanding of grammar rules and improved writing skills.

Grammarly also offers suggestions to improve the style and tone of your writing, making it more engaging and appropriate for your audience. This can be particularly helpful in understanding the nuances of formal versus informal writing.

This, for example, helped Jeb shift from a passive to an active writing style, which is more direct, clear, and engaging. Readers can't always pinpoint what they like about writing or why, but they definitely know it when they read it. Case in point: the shift to active voice had a positive impact on his book sales.

By actively engaging with the feedback and suggestions provided by Grammarly, along with the awareness you gain from reading books like *On Writing Well*, you can quickly improve your writing skills.

EXERCISE 20.1: IDENTIFY THREE AREAS OF YOUR WRITING TO IMPROVE

Take a moment to consider your writing, especially business writing. Make a list of the aspects you'd like to improve (e.g., more concise, warmer tone, more varied sentences, better flow, improved syntax, clearer organization, etc.). Now circle the three areas you'd like to focus on first.

Once you know what you want to change, you can pay particular attention to those elements as you write. Better yet, you can use AI to hone those areas of your work. Chapter 21 will cover how to develop prompts to focus AI's attention on specific edits. Working on no more than three at a time will also help you develop your skills.

EXERCISE 20.2: YOU VERSUS ROBOT

In this exercise you will compare your writing style to your robot.

Step One: Choose a subject.

Step Two: Write 500 words on that subject.

Step Three: Give ChatGPT or Claude this prompt: "Write a 500-word article on [your chosen subject]."

Step Four: Compare your writing style to the robot's output.

Step Five: Make a note of what you can improve in your writing. Consider how you might edit the robot's writing to make sure your final result has a human touch, even if it draws on the robot's strengths.

21

The Power of Editing

Between the two of us we've written over two million words. What we've learned through more than 10,000 hours of practice is that books are shaped during the editing process, not the writing process. It's just as Michelangelo said: "The sculpture is already complete within the marble block, before I start my work. It is already there, I just have to chisel away the superfluous material."

Human writing is messy and imperfect. Robot writing is boring and stiff. Editing makes what you and your robot write readable. It's about chiseling away all of the superfluous words in order to present the reader with information that makes sense, is easy to consume, and is pleasurable to read.

The primary reason you need to study writing is because it makes you a better editor. You need to be able to:

1. Edit yourself without AI.

2. Write prompts that help your AI edit you.

3. Proof and edit your AI.

Editing is primarily about taking words out, improving the arrangement, and simplifying the text. It's where the magic happens. AI tools like Wordrake can help with this process.

The biggest mistake that most people make with their own writing and AI writing is that they don't edit because doing so is hard, tedious, and time consuming. But when you skip editing, the result is sloppy, poorly organized writing that makes you look lazy and stupid.

Resolve now to be disciplined with editing before you allow AI to help you with writing.

Your Superhuman Editor

Written language and grammar are complicated. It's impossible for most normal humans to remember how and when to apply all the rules, much less how words are spelled. We tend to botch basic grammar, verb tense, and prepositions. We also tend to write long, verbose sentences rather than getting to the point.

The rules of grammar don't always make sense and sometimes shift with context. Consider this one that you likely learned in school: "I before E except after C." This is where AI, as an editor and proofreader, shines (see what AI has to say about this rule on the next page). It has consumed all of the rules, knows how words are spelled, and has the ability to proof your written documents at superhuman speeds.

Mastering Editing Prompts

The key to leveraging AI as your editor is knowing how to prompt it to do the job. Engineering a prompt that will look for grammar mistakes like verb tense and prepositions will improve your written communication without making you less human. Here's an example of a complex editing prompt for a formal sales proposal:

ChatGPT

The rule "I before E except after C" is a mnemonic that helps in spelling words in English where the combination of the letters "i" and "e" can be confusing. It suggests that in words where the "i" and "e" are together, the correct order is usually "ie," unless they follow the letter "c," in which case the correct order is "ei."

However, there are numerous exceptions to this rule, and these exceptions can be categorized as follows:

1. **Words where 'ei' does not follow a 'c':** There are many words where "ei" appears without a preceding "c" and does not make the "ee" sound, like "neither," "weird," "protein," and "height."
2. **Words where 'ie' follows a 'c':** Some words have "ie" after a "c" and still follow the rule, such as "species," "science," and "sufficient."
3. **Words with a different pronunciation:** The rule is primarily based on pronunciation. When "ei" or "ie" makes a sound different from "ee," the rule does not apply. For instance, in words like "efficient" and "ancient," the "ie/ei" makes an "i" sound.
4. **Foreign or borrowed words:** English includes many words from other languages that don't follow its spelling conventions. Words like "leisure" (from French) do not conform to the rule.

Due to these numerous exceptions, the "I before E except after C" rule is often criticized for being more confusing than helpful. It's more of a general guideline than an absolute rule, and learning the specific spelling of words is usually more effective.

"Please thoroughly spell-check and review the grammar in the following sales proposal text. It's intended for a formal business context, so I need the language to be professional and polished. Pay special attention to technical terms and industry jargon to ensure they are correctly used and spelled. Also, please check for consistency in terminology and formatting, especially in product names and technical specifications. I'm targeting an American English audience, so make sure the spelling conforms to American English standards. Lastly, if there are any sentences that could be rephrased for clarity or persuasiveness, I would appreciate your suggestions. Here's the text: [Insert Sales Proposal Text Here]."

This prompt clearly indicates the need for a thorough spell-check, grammar review, and style considerations in a specific professional context, ensuring the language used is appropriate and effective for its intended purpose.

Here are a couple more editing prompts just for fun:

- **Robert Gottlieb prompt:** "You are the editor Robert Gottlieb and you have decided to help a salesperson improve their writing. You will edit the text for spelling errors, missing words, grammar or syntax problems, and tone. You will only make changes to the text when there is a problem."

- **Benjamin Dreyer prompt:** "You are the editor Benjamin Dreyer, copy chief at Random House, and you have decided to help a salesperson improve their writing. You will edit the text for spelling errors, missing words, grammar or syntax problems, and tone. You will only make changes to the text when there is a problem."

A word of caution. Sometimes AI will make edits and changes to your sentences that make it obvious that your writing was edited by a robot. For this reason, it is important that you proofread your documents after AI finishes its edits. If something doesn't sound natural, change it.

Punctuation

Some of the biggest mistakes sales professionals make with written communication are punctuation mistakes. It is easy to use commas, apostrophes, and semicolons the wrong way, in the wrong place, or with the wrong context.

- **Comma problem:** "Our company, is releasing a new product this month." The comma isn't necessary.

- **Apostrophe problem:** "Get your's before we run out." *Your's* should be *yours*.
- **Semicolon problem:** "This solution is our best; because it's the highest quality and the lowest cost." No need for a semicolon.

You could take a course on English grammar and spend your time diagramming sentences until you are a world-class editor. Or you could ask your AI to do the work for you and review your writing for punctuation mistakes, as in this punctuation prompt:

> "Please review this document for punctuation errors. Correct any mistakes you find, including those related to commas, periods, semicolons, colons, apostrophes, quotation marks, and any other punctuation. Ensure that the sentences are grammatically correct and the meaning is clear."

Then paste the content of your document following this prompt. Break longer documents into smaller sections and check each section one at a time to ensure accuracy and thoroughness.

Vocabulary

How you use vocabulary significantly influences how people perceive you. The effective use of vocabulary in written communication is crucial for conveying your message accurately, establishing credibility, engaging the reader, and evoking the desired emotional response. It plays a vital role in how your writing is perceived and received by your audience.

- Have you ever used *pole* when you meant to use *poll*? I don't even have to ask if you have ever used *there* when you meant *their*. These words are homonyms, so they sound the same but have different meanings. Getting them switched up can lead to embarrassing moments.

- When we want to sound smart, we have a tendency to use 5-dollar words when a 25-cent word will do, like saying, "a preponderance of our clients" instead of "most of our clients."

- We are all guilty of using the same words over and over in our writing. Varied vocabulary makes your writing more engaging and interesting, helps to hold the reader's attention longer, and makes your text more memorable. For example, the idea of being *consultative* could be conveyed by using *advisory, guiding, informing,* or *recommending.* Your company could be your *firm, business, enterprise,* or *corporation.* Your solution could be your *offering, products, approach, resolution,* or *answer.*

Poor vocabulary can cause you to seem uneducated, stiff, boring, pompous, or repetitive. Well-chosen vocabulary conveys your message with clarity and makes your writing robust, authentic, and readable.

- **Clarity and precision:** The right words effectively convey complex ideas, making it easier for the reader to understand your message. This is particularly important in sales writing.

- **Tone and style:** The right vocabulary sets the appropriate tone for your audience. For example, using formal or sophisticated words can make your writing sound more professional, while simpler, colloquial language can make it more accessible, authentic, and relatable.

- **Credibility and authority:** Using appropriate and accurate vocabulary can enhance your credibility. It demonstrates knowledge and confidence in the subject matter, leading readers to trust and respect your perspective more, which is crucial in sales.

- **Emotional impact:** Words have the power to evoke emotions. The right words can help you persuade readers to buy your ideas.

- **Avoiding misunderstandings:** Precise vocabulary helps in avoiding ambiguities and misunderstandings. Especially in sensitive or complex topics, the right words can ensure your message is interpreted as intended.

With a simple prompt, AI can improve your vocabulary and create greater variety in your writing. It will call out words that have been used incorrectly and make your writing easier to read. It will also help you flex your vocabulary to the context and for your intended audience.

For example, to make it easier for your reader to understand, ask AI to rewrite the text for someone with a tenth-grade reading level. You can also ask AI to remove anything that might cause a conflict by asking it to make the text more diplomatic to avoid offending people.

Here are six prompts for editing vocabulary:

1. **Enhance vocabulary for professional tone:** "Please review this document and enhance the vocabulary to make it sound more professional. Replace any informal or colloquial language with more formal and sophisticated words where appropriate."

2. **Simplify vocabulary for clarity:** "I want this document to be easily understandable to a general audience. Please simplify the vocabulary, replacing complex or technical terms with more common and accessible language."

3. **Subject-specific vocabulary enhancement:** "This document is related to [subject, topic, industry]. Please revise it to include more subject-specific vocabulary and terms that are commonly used in this field to make it more authoritative."

4. **Vocabulary diversification:** "Can you edit this document to diversify the vocabulary? I'm looking to make the writing more engaging and avoid repetitive language. Please introduce synonyms and varied expressions where possible."

5. **Influence:** "This piece is meant to [evoke a specific emotion, e.g., inspire, persuade, excite]. Please modify the vocabulary to enhance the emotional impact of the writing, using words that effectively convey the desired feeling."

6. **Word replacement:** "You are an editor with a focus on varying word usage to improve the writing by replacing words that appear too frequently in a text. You are conservative, choosing well-known words instead of words that might make it difficult for the reader."

You'll get even better results from these prompts when you provide context or specific instructions about your target audience or the purpose of the document.

Spelling

If you want to embarrass yourself in front of your prospect or customer, misspelling words will do it. I am not throwing the first stone; all I need to do is misspell a word on a newsletter to be flooded with emails pointing out the error. As you know, it isn't helpful to discover a misspelled word *after* you've sent a well-crafted email or delivered your final proposal for the biggest deal you've ever pursued.

While it's not a big deal for every customer, someone may have second thoughts if they believe you are sloppy and not good with the details. I know several buyers who are perfectionists and will not buy from salespeople who have misspelled words and typos in their presentations and proposals.

While you should certainly use the spell-check function that is embedded in most email clients and platforms like Microsoft Office and Google Docs, AI takes spell-checking to a whole new level. Creating effective spell-check prompts for AI platforms like ChatGPT, though, involves clearly identifying the text that needs to be checked and specifying your expectations for the correction.

Here are some best practices for crafting spell-check prompts:

- **Specify the text clearly:** Clearly indicate the text you want to be spell-checked. You can say something like, "Please spell-check the following text: [Your Text Here]."
- **Contextual spell-checking:** If you need spell-checking in a specific context (like formal writing, proposal documents, etc.), mention it. For example, try something like "Can you spell-check this paragraph for a sales proposal written for a C-level audience?"
- **Check for common errors:** Ask specifically for checks on common mistakes if needed, like homophones, grammar, or punctuation, such as "Please check this email for any spelling and grammar errors."
- **Word or phrase focus:** If you're unsure about a particular word or phrase, point it out. "Is the spelling of 'accommodate' correct in this context?"
- **Consider language variants:** If you're using a specific variant of English (like British, American, or Australian), specify which one for accurate spelling checks. "Can you spell-check this text according to British English standards?"
- **Request for explanation:** If you want to understand the reason behind the corrections, ask for it. "Please spell-check

the following text and explain why changes are made." This is an excellent way to learn and improve your spelling and vocabulary.

- **Check for consistency:** If your text contains names, technical terms, or specific jargon, ask for consistency checks. "Please ensure that all the technical terms in this text are spelled consistently."
- **Proofreading beyond spelling:** If you want more than just spelling checks, like style and tone, mention that. Say, "Please spell-check this text and suggest improvements for a more formal tone."

When you create prompts that are clear and precise, it enables your AI to provide more accurate and helpful spell-checking assistance.

Sentence Structure

Humans tend to write long, compound sentences that are difficult to understand. Anthony's editor once told him that if something could be said in 500 words, he could easily do it in 1500. Since then, he has been on a quest to express his ideas in shorter, more concise sentences.

Most of the time, long sentences are the result of a stream-of-consciousness writing process. When writing down your thoughts as they come, sentences can become long and winding. This style reflects the way thoughts often flow in the human mind—not always in neat, concise packages. However, it's hard for anyone to follow another person's thoughts when they're put to paper without any editorial considerations. If you don't spend enough time refining your writing and streamlining your sentences, ideas tend to remain disorganized and wordy.

It's important to note that neither long nor short sentences are inherently superior; effective writing often involves a balance of both. When varying sentence length, tailor your approach to the purpose of the communication and the needs of the audience. Overusing short sentences can make the text feel choppy or simplistic, but run-on sentences can lose the reader and obscure your meaning. A mix of sentence lengths is often best, as it can make the writing more dynamic and interesting. The key is to use shorter sentences strategically to enhance your writing and communicate your ideas effectively.

Still, shorter sentences in written communication are considered more effective than longer ones, especially in business writing.

- Short sentences are generally more direct and easier to understand. Each sentence can deliver a single idea or concept, reducing the cognitive load on the reader and making it easier to digest the information.
- In an age of information overload, shorter sentences can help maintain the reader's attention. They make the text appear less daunting, encouraging the reader to continue reading.
- Short sentences can quicken the pace of your writing, creating a sense of urgency or excitement. They can also vary the rhythm of your text, which can help keep the reader engaged.
- A short sentence, especially when used after a series of longer ones, stands out and can be used to emphasize a point. It can make an impact, drawing the reader's focus to key information or ideas.
- Readers are less likely to misinterpret short sentences.
- Short sentences can make a text more accessible, especially for readers with varying levels of language proficiency or

those reading in a non-native language. They also cater well to the reading habits of people browsing on mobile devices.

- Simple, concise sentences are easier to remember. When you communicate key points in short sentences, readers are more likely to retain what you say.

The good news is that AI can help you both shorten your sentences and create variety in your writing. All you need to do is give it the right (not write) prompt.

Here are six prompts for editing sentence length and variety:

- **Shortening for clarity and variety:** "Please review this document and shorten any overly long sentences. Aim for a mix of short and long sentences to enhance clarity and maintain reader engagement. Break down complex sentences where necessary and vary sentence length to improve readability."

- **Balancing sentence length:** "I'd like this document to have a balanced flow. Please identify and break up any long sentences into shorter ones where appropriate. Also, ensure there's a good mix of short, medium, and long sentences throughout to create a pleasing rhythm."

- **Simplifying for a broader audience:** "This document needs to be more accessible to a general audience. Please simplify it by shortening long sentences and breaking up complex ideas into smaller, more digestible parts. However, retain a few longer sentences where they add value or are necessary for conveying specific details."

- **Enhancing readability and flow:** "Review this document for readability. Focus on shortening sentences that are too long and cumbersome, but also integrate some longer sentences to maintain a natural and engaging flow. The goal is to make the text easy to read while keeping it interesting and dynamic."

- **Streamlining for efficiency:** "Please edit this document to make it more concise and efficient. Shorten lengthy sentences and eliminate unnecessary words. However, ensure that the document still contains a variety of sentence lengths to maintain an engaging and professional tone."
- **Verlyn Klinkenborg prompt:** "You are Verlyn Klinkenborg, a member of the editorial board of the *New York Times*. You have been hired to make this text easier to read by shortening the sentences that are longer than they should be."

These prompts guide the editing process toward creating a document with a balanced mix of sentence lengths, enhancing both clarity and engagement.

Teaching Your Robot What Not to Do

AI is like Flavor Flav. It is a hype machine, though without the clock around its neck. It can be like one of Jeb's thoroughbred horses. Even though you are holding the reins, the horse will sometimes choose its own direction, ignoring the well-constructed prompt you built.

For this reason, you may have to tame your AI to soften the hype or follow your prompt with rules that tell it what not to do. Giving your robot a list of what to avoid helps rein in its tendency to run away with your prompt and choose its own path. For example, "Do not rewrite my text unless there is a spelling mistake, a missing word, a grammar problem, a syntax issue, or a punctuation error."

Here is an example of a how a ChatGPT dialogue flows best:

- **"Don't" prompt:** "Don't rewrite my text unless there is a misspelled word, a missing word, a grammar issue, a syntax issue, or a punctuation problem. Don't reduce the word count. When changing a word, make sure it is at a tenth-grade level. Will you please follow these rules?"

- **Once AI responds in the affirmative, enter the "Do" prompt:** Once you have forbidden the AI from doing what you don't want, give it a list of what you do want it to do. "Please write in the active voice. Write in the first person. Shorten any long sentences or rewrite any sentence that has two or more commas, and limit it to a single comma. Adjust the text for an audience of business leaders. Remove any word that isn't necessary to help streamline the text. Provide a table of edits you made. Will you please follow these rules?"

- **Once AI responds in the affirmative:** Upload your document or paste your text.

Your results will be better when you give your robot strong direction on what you don't want it to do and what you want it to avoid. If, for some reason, something isn't working as you intended, stay in your current chat and ask it to stop doing the things you don't like.

Remember that you are chatting with your robot in a single conversation. Keep chatting with your AI in that conversation because it will retain the instructions you've already given it. Starting a new chat is essentially starting over from scratch.

22

AI Is a Faster Writer; You Are a Better Human

A *I writes content fast. Just type: "Write an article about [name* *a subject]." You'll have an article in about 30 seconds. It's* *truly magical!*

But before you start celebrating how AI is going to lift the burden of writing off of your shoulders, go back and read the opening story in Chapter 19. AI can write fast, but most of the time the writing is bland, stiff, and stuffed with cringy, easy-to-spot robot patterns.

With this, we are back to the original premise of this book. You gain the AI Edge when you use AI to enhance your human advantage rather than to replace it. AI can write content from scratch faster than you, but not better than you.

The more you use AI for generating content, the more you'll notice that it repeats itself. These patterns make robot-generated text easy to spot, which can damage your credibility and relationships. The last thing you want is a client who can recognize you did nothing more than copy and paste what your robot provided you.

Humans write better because we are asymmetric, imperfect, and more interesting. Because you are a human communicating with other humans, you need to edit what AI writes so that it remains grammatically correct but feels like you wrote it. This means you may need to change out words that you would never use—unless, of course, you are writing for your English literature professor. (In this case, for fun, you might ask AI to "write in the style of Shakespeare.")

Speed up the Editing Process by Teaching AI to Sound More Human

First, let's acknowledge that this takes time, and you want to move faster. To speed up the editing process you can teach your AI, through prompts, how to write more like a human, including you. Use these 10 prompts[1] to reduce the robospeak and make what AI writes sound more human:

1. Vary sentence structure; embrace asymmetry.
2. Mix formal and informal tones.
3. Avoid repetitive points or phrases.
4. Include personal stories or perspectives.
5. Be specific and detailed, not generic.
6. Write with emotional depth.
7. Introduce natural imperfections in the writing.

---

[1] These ten prompts are courtesy of our friend Joe Mullen, https://www.linkedin.com/in/mullenjoseph/.

8. Use simple, conversational sentence structures.

9. Avoid keyword stuffing; use terms naturally.

10. Balance facts with interpretive insights.

Speed up the Editing Process by Teaching AI to Sound More Like You

Another exciting way to speed up the process of editing what your robot writes is to teach it how to use your voice. Once you do this, the content it creates will sound much more natural and more like the way you would say it.

You'll still need to edit to remove the robot patterns, but this will shorten the process considerably. This is what you do:

Step One: Start by gathering five articles or documents you've written that you consider your best work (be sure that others concur). For best results you'll want to collect 1000–2000 words in total.

Step Two: Convert the text into a single PDF, then upload into your preferred AI.

Step Three: Use this prompt: "Assume you are an expert ghostwriter specializing in linguistics and natural language processing. Analyze the provided text and convert it into a detailed style guide, reflecting the author's writing style, voice, tone, structure, and other distinguishing characteristics. Output in bullet points."

Step Four: Review the style guide that AI produces and decide what you wish to keep and what to discard.

Step Five: Use this style guide in your writing prompts. "Please follow these style guidelines in your response: *Voice*: [*Your Description*], *Tone*: [*Your Description*], *Style*: [*Your Description*], *Structure*: [*Your Description*]."

While AI can adapt to your style, it may not perfectly adhere to all the intricacies of your personal style guide, especially in a single interaction. Constantly interacting with AI using your desired style or pointing out when the style needs to be adjusted can gradually steer the responses in the right direction. By using this approach, your AI-generated content becomes more you, and you gain back time to sell more.

AUTHORS' NOTE

The output doesn't belong to you. At the time of this writing only humans may copyright original work. AI is not a human, so if you are using generative AI, the output does not belong to you. Even though we could have used prompts to write this book, we used human hands and minds to craft it, and our publisher will ensure this book has a copyright. Damn straight!

If you are writing something that isn't important or strategic enough that you wouldn't worry about someone stealing it and using it for their own purposes, you don't have to worry about a copyright. If you use AI to help you with something you wouldn't want to fall into your competitor's possession, you should only share it with your client or your sales team.

PART 5
Prospecting

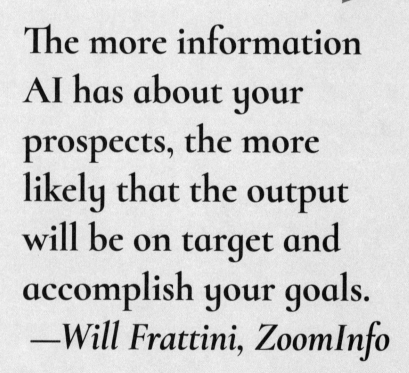

The more information AI has about your prospects, the more likely that the output will be on target and accomplish your goals.
—*Will Frattini, ZoomInfo*

23

The Asynchronous Seller

T he inside sales professional I was coaching had been
underperforming for a while. The year before, on a team of
30 inside sales reps, he'd been a top performer and made it to the
President's Club. Recently, however, his productivity had dropped
off, and it had not recovered.

We were sitting face-to-face at one corner of a large
conference table. I asked questions to diagnose his performance
problem over the last few months—a problem that, despite the
evidence, he denied he had. It was the sad delusion of an
underperformer.

I asked him to walk me through his day and describe his
outbound prospecting process. I sat back in my chair in disbelief
as he told me that his entire prospecting methodology was
sending out hundreds of AI-generated emails to prospects from
his sales engagement platform each day.

Seeing the "Oh shit, I can't believe you just said that" look
on my face, he defended this practice. "It works," he said, while

barely hiding the defensive tone in his voice. "People respond to my emails looking for more information."

For a few more minutes, I let him talk in circles, listening to him justify why he wasn't talking with people. Then I interrupted him. "Eric, here's the thing. If you're telling me that sending emails is the most effective means of engaging buyers and closing business, then we don't need you. It would be a lot cheaper to just let the robot do your job."

The look on his face was that of a hurt puppy that had just been whacked with a rolled-up newspaper for peeing on the floor. But I could see the wheels turning as he tried to cobble together a response. "I'm really offended you'd say that," he shot back.

"Well," I responded, "I'm really offended you're collecting a $75,000-a-year salary to do what a $19-a-month robot can do better than you."

Once I was able to get his attention and shake him out of his delusion, we were able to get him back on track. But he almost got fired because he forgot that his job was to use his human advantage to talk with people.

False Promises, Lies, and Bullshit

As a rule, salespeople hate prospecting; hence the overwhelming hype and promises that AI will remove that burden. The companies behind AI platforms claim that their technology will move us into a utopian age of sales in which there is no pain and all gain.

- **Promise:** AI can be programmed to mimic your voice and leave personalized prospecting voice messages. Just type the message and the robot does all the work. Leave hundreds of voice messages for prospects with little to no effort. (This experiment will end badly.)

- **Promise:** An AI video version of you will create personalized video prospecting messages with the push of a button. (Cool, but wickedly creepy and also doomed to fail.)
- **Promise:** AI will take over outbound cold calling with real-time calls to your prospects that mimic your voice. (Another experiment that will end badly, considering how much people hate talking to robots.)
- **Promise:** AI can be programmed to automatically build and send personalized prospecting email and social media direct messages at scale. These messages will fill your pipeline with qualified opportunities with almost no effort on your part. (Already ending badly.)

Tech entrepreneurs know that salespeople don't like prospecting and that leaders often lack the courage and know-how to lead, manage, and coach prospecting activities. They exploit your desire for an easy button with promises that their new applications will make prospecting effortless.

The charlatans say that their AI platforms will automate cold calling and fill your pipeline to the brim with high-quality opportunities. They promise, "Our AI tool will take over the heavy lifting so that your salespeople will never have to cold call again." *This is bullshit—an outright lie.*

This is the snake oil of our time. AI platforms and tech companies will keep coming back with the same promises. They will tell you that their bots will make prospecting easy and painless, and you will buy it because easy is the most powerful of all marketing hooks, especially with something like prospecting, which people don't like to do.

Get Right with Reality

AI is a powerful tool that will help you become more effective and efficient at prospecting, but it will not remove your responsibility to interrupt and talk with people. It is not an easy button. Not a panacea. Not a replacement for the human touch.

Reality: When you allow AI to take the place of *you*, things will get worse for you, not better. Yes, an AI tool will write emails and direct messages, leave voice messages, and create videos. But people will intuitively know that these messages are AI generated.

As we discussed in Chapter 19, when people find out they are dealing with a robot and not you, it turns them off. It breaks trust. They will ignore, delete, and block you. People don't like to be manipulated, they do not like conversing with robots, and they lose respect for you when it becomes clear that you invested no effort in the work to pursue them.

Worse, when thousands of sales organizations and millions of salespeople use this approach, it causes every salesperson's asynchronous prospecting messages to become suspect. This is exactly why Google has instituted a massive change in how they rate incoming emails. Their new approach punishes senders who flood inboxes indiscriminately with automated AI garbage.

When you or your company sign up for too-good-to-be-true AI solutions, you are putting your brand and personal reputation at risk. You may also be putting your web domain at risk of being permanently blocked. A better use of this money is to take it out into your front parking lot and light it on fire.

There Is No Easy Button for Prospecting

Let's get real. The number-one reason for failure in sales is an empty pipeline, and the root cause of an empty pipeline is that salespeople fail to consistently prospect for new opportunities. But you and pretty much every red-blooded salesperson on the planet already know this.

- You know that you need to be disciplined, relentless, and fanatical.

- You know that you need to talk to people.
- You know that you need to prioritize prospecting activity each sales day.
- You know, as Jeb says, "The pipe is life."

But you don't do it. You are hit and miss. Hot and cold. Inconsistent. You prospect hard when your pipeline is empty and you are under pressure, and you take your foot off the accelerator and become complacent when you are closing sales.

Meanwhile, because your prospecting activity is inconsistent, your income is inconsistent and you are stressed out most of the time. This is when you become susceptible to easy-button hype and bullshit lies.

Nothing is more important to your success in sales than prospecting. Nothing. This is where the rubber meets the road. The more people you talk with, the more your pipeline will grow, the more sales you will make, and the more you will earn.

If you want success in sales you must become a relentless, unstoppable, fanatical prospector who is obsessive about keeping your pipeline full of qualified prospects. Prospecting must become the air you breathe.

Prospect day and night, anywhere and anytime. You must always be on the hunt for your next sale. Carry around a pocket full of business cards. Strike up conversations with strangers in line to get coffee, in elevators, on planes, trains, and anywhere else you can talk with people and qualify potential prospects. Ask people where they work, what they do, and who makes decisions at their company.

Get up in the morning and bang the phone. During the day, knock on doors. Go to networking events, invest in your professional network. At night build your personal brand and engage prospects on social media. Before you quit for the day, make even more calls. Don't even think for a minute that there is an AI easy button that's going to do it for you!

24

Synchronous versus Asynchronous Prospecting

To succeed in modern selling, you must become adept at prospecting and communicating through a complex web of interconnected communication channels—synchronous and asynchronous—often at the same time. Interconnected is the key word. There isn't one best way. Communication channels are not siloed.

There are two primary forms of prospecting communication that you need to master and learn to blend together (interconnect) to be effective:

1. **Synchronous is talking with people in real time:** These communication channels—primarily telephone and

in-person and secondarily text and direct messaging—are dynamic and require both parties to be available and engaged in the conversation at the same time.

2. **Asynchronous is talking at people, independent of time:** These communication channels—including email, voice messaging, video messaging, and direct messaging—do not require both parties to be available and engaged at the same time.

Viva la Synchronous Prospecting

Prospecting is the art of *interrupting*—primarily through synchronous channels and secondarily through asynchronous channels. Prospecting is straightforward and tactical. It's about moving opportunities into your pipeline now and qualifying prospects for the future.

In today's digital world, it's easy to avoid talking to people. It's easy to justify that the people who buy from you would like to avoid talking with you, too.

Talking with people—synchronous prospecting—is difficult. You must pay attention, listen, and flex your communication style. You must put the other person at the center of your attention. It can make you vulnerable and expose you to the potential for rejection.

Most salespeople should be blocking time daily (preferably first thing in the morning) for synchronous prospecting because it is the shortest, most direct path to creating new pipeline opportunities. To be effective, you need:

- A list of targeted prospects
- Effective sales messaging to grab their attention and compel them to engage

- A blend of channels—phone, in-person, email, direct messaging, text messaging, video messaging, social media, snail mail
- Objection turnaround scripts
- A well-designed, multi-touch prospecting sequence

To hit home runs in sales you need to be the interrupter, not the "interruptee." Of course, when you interrupt people, they push back, which is why synchronous prospecting is such rejection-dense work.

This is exactly why thousands of misguided salespeople have deluded themselves into thinking that using automated tools to effortlessly send thousands of emails "personalized" with AI is good enough. (It is not.)

This behavior is why so many sales floors are dead silent. It is why so many sales teams and organizations are woefully behind their forecasts and business plans. It's transacting versus engaging. It's why so many buyers are left longing for real human-to-human interaction.

It's also a big reason why there are so many new tech companies popping up that claim they can replace your sales team with an AI-driven software application. They are partially right. If all you do is send emails all day long, you can be replaced. Robots are not that great at complex, real-time conversations, but they are pretty good at sending cheesy, awkwardly personalized prospecting emails at scale.

If we learn nothing else from the great coronavirus pandemic, it's that real human connection matters. And you are just not going to get that from an AI-generated email.

The more complex the sale, the longer the sales cycle, the higher the dollar amount, the greater the risk to the stakeholders, and the more emotions are involved in the decision to purchase, the more companies need salespeople who are intelligent, creative, insightful, influential, and persuasive to shift win probabilities in the organization's favor. And the more they need you to talk with people.

Talk with People

There is a fundamental formula for sustained sales success: The more people you talk with, the more you will sell. Talking with people is what we, as sales professionals, get paid to do. It's just that simple. Synchronous prospecting is where you earn your chops as a sales professional.

There is no doubt that asynchronous communication channels have an important place in prospecting. These channels allow you to move fast and communicate when you are unable to connect with your prospect in real time.

The problem is that AI-automated mass emails, voicemails, videos, and direct messages—and the follow-on tech tools to combat this spam—will eventually kill most *asynchronous* prospecting because no one will trust it. This is causing a massive reawakening of the art of real-time phone and in-person prospecting calls.

The bad news is that, despite all of the promises that the tech companies make, AI can't do the talking for you, no matter how badly you might wish it to be so. What AI can't do, and should not do, is pretend that it is human. It is your job to connect with prospects on a human level. This is your human advantage.

25

A Powerful
Prospecting Partner

Now that we've broken the bad news that there is no AI easy button, and that despite the promises you'll still need to talk with people, let's discuss the good news.

Artificial intelligence is a powerful prospecting partner that, combined with your human intelligence, will help you keep your pipeline full. What AI can do very well is help you target who you should be talking with and provide you with research, background summaries and dossiers, questions to ask during conversations, and intent data. All of which helps you engage the right people in more meaningful conversations. Here are some of the other things that AI can do for you:

- Automating repetitive tasks
- Scheduling and reminding
- Mapping for in-person prospecting

- Data mining and intent gathering
- Building targeted prospecting lists
- Improving your efficiency and effectiveness with research
- Crafting better messaging
- Developing content for slow prospecting activities
- Managing prospecting sequences

At a minimum, AI will give you more time to prospect more. Fully integrated into your prospecting workflow, it will help you target the right prospects, at the right time, with the right message, giving you a decisive competitive advantage in gaining the attention of and engaging highly qualified prospects in your market.

Get to Know Your AI-Driven Prospecting Tools

In previous chapters we've shared prompts for combining your human advantage with AI's edge. With prospecting, prompts can certainly help you with developing messaging and research. However, the majority of the AI tools you'll be using for prospecting activities are being built directly into your CRM, sales engagement platform, and social media platforms like LinkedIn, among others.

Therefore, it is crucial that you get to know these tools and practice with them now. You need to gain an understanding of their limitations, where they can help or hurt you, and how you can adapt them to your prospecting motions.

All of these tools will be constantly evolving. As soon as a new AI feature is added, jump in and figure it out. Learn how to prompt and give direction to the AI in your core sales platforms. Play with it and work with it until you become adept at using AI to help you elevate, amplify, and accelerate your prospecting game.

26

Prospecting Sequences

When prospects don't know you, it's much harder to get them to engage. Because prospects are being deluged with AI-generated prospecting spam, it's an even bigger challenge.

As the adage goes, "Attention is currency." In an era characterized by diminished attention spans, capturing someone's attention is akin to striking gold. For salespeople, this couldn't be truer.

This is where prospecting sequences come into play. Prospecting sequences systematize and organize persistence to give you an edge over your competitors when vying for the limited attention of prospects.

A prospecting sequence is an intentional series of prospecting touches, cross-leveraging multiple communication channels to improve the probability of compelling your prospect to engage. Sometimes your first prospecting message misses the mark. A prospecting sequence also allows you to try multiple iterations of your message to home in on something that is relevant enough for your prospect to agree to meet with you.

Sequences help you grab attention through a series of interconnected messages that, over time, build familiarity. Familiarity leads to liking. The more a prospect hears and sees your name, your company, and your message, the more familiar you become to them, and the more likely you are to grab their attention and compel them to engage.

Managing the Complexity of Prospecting Sequences

Running effective prospecting sequences is complex. There are a lot of moving parts. This is where AI shines because AI manages complexity far better than humans.

Think about prospecting sequences like an intricate ballet where every touchpoint is a step, a movement designed to engage, educate, build familiarity, and ultimately convert prospects into customers. This is where AI steps in, acting as the choreographer behind the scenes, ensuring every move is executed to perfection while managing CRM updates, task reminders, calendars, and administrative tasks on the backend.

The administrative burden of managing multitouch sequences can also be time consuming. AI simplifies this by automating tasks such as scheduling next steps and updating CRM records. This frees you up to focus on what you do best: engaging in synchronous conversations with prospects.

Seven Elements of Effective Prospecting

As outlined in Jeb's 2022 book, *Selling in a Crisis: 55 Ways to Stay Motivated and Increase Sales in Volatile Times*, there are seven elements of prospecting sequences:

1. Targeting
2. Messaging
3. Channels

4. Cadence

5. Touches

6. Duration

7. Spacing

The formula for success with prospecting sequences is simple:

$$(\text{Targeted List} + \text{Right Channels} + \text{Right Time}) \times \text{Compelling Messaging} = \text{Conversion}$$

Building and running effective sequences can be a daunting task. They are complex and it is hard to know if the sequence you're running is the right one for your targeted list.

The good news is that in big ways and small ways, the AI tools that are being built into your CRM and sales engagement platforms can make it much easier to develop and execute effective prospecting sequences.

Managing sequences effectively requires a deep commitment to mastering targeting, timing, channel techniques, and message relevance. AI can transform your sequences, making them more strategic, personalized, and adaptable.

As you review each element, take a moment to consider the AI tools you have at your disposal now, both built into your core sales platforms and independent of those platforms, that you can plug into to power up your prospecting efforts. At the end of this chapter, we've included an exercise to help you inventory these tools and how you might leverage them to help you execute more effective prospecting sequences.

Targeted Lists and Messaging

Effective sequences begin and end with targeted lists. Get dialed in on your ideal customer profile (ICP), industry vertical, geography, or decision-making role. The better and more targeted your list, the better your prospecting outcomes.

Messaging

Message matters. It is the most important part of the prospecting sequencing equation. It is also the most challenging and time-consuming step. Poorly thought out messaging and setting-it-and-forgetting-it with AI is why most prospecting sequences fail.

Targeting and messaging are areas in which AI can give you wings. We'll dive deeper into these important elements in subsequent chapters.

Communication Channels

A multichannel prospecting approach improves the probability (over a single siloed approach) that you meet prospects where they are and how they prefer to communicate. Therefore, it is crucial to choose the right set of channels for each targeted list and applied sequence.

Channels include:

- Phone
- In-person
- Email
- Voice messaging
- Direct messaging
- Video messaging
- Text messaging
- Social media engagement
- Snail mail

If you are more comfortable with a particular channel— especially an asynchronous channel—shake yourself out of that comfort zone. The interwoven, cross-channel approach is crucial to bending statistical probability in your favor that prospects engage.

However, for best results running multichannel sequences, we highly recommend that you invest in a sequencing/sales engagement platform such as Salesloft, Apollo, Gong, Outreach, or VanillaSoft if your CRM does not have a built-in sequencing functionality. These tools will become even more powerful as AI continues to evolve.

Sequencing and sales engagement is a big business. But it also has a big problem. These platforms are intended to help salespeople with multithread communication channels across their sequences. Instead, they have been bastardized by those same salespeople into very expensive email spam bots used to avoid talking with people.

Sending automated email should *never* become the primary purpose of your sequencing tool. Though email should continue to be part of your sequences, it should not be the star of the show.

Instead, your sequence should guide multiple touches across a multithread of communication channels, using interwoven messages, with an emphasis on synchronous channels like the phone and in-person that allow you to have real-time conversations with prospects.

Cadence and Touches

The cadence is the order of your prospecting touches within the sequence, by channel. For example:

Phone > Voice Message > Email > LinkedIn >
Video Message > Snail Mail > Direct Message (in that order)

The ultimate objective of a prospecting sequence is to engage a prospect in a conversation.

A big mistake that salespeople make is starting sequences with an asynchronous channel like email, rather than a synchronous channel like the phone, which gives them the best chance of actually talking with their prospects.

Far too often cadences are front-loaded with asynchronous channels to "warm prospects up" before a call is ever made. This is wrong. The focus of your cadence is to improve the probability of engaging prospects in conversations as early in the sequence as possible.

When sequences are front-loaded with synchronous attempts, you will engage more prospects, in less time, with better outcomes. Better yet, when you get your prospect on the phone or face to face and talk with them on your first attempt, then you don't need a complex 18-touch prospecting sequence run by your AI. Just dial the number, knock on the door, have a conversation, and keep moving.

Touches

Once you've settled on the prospecting channels for your sequence, and the order in which those channels will be deployed, the next step is to choose how many prospecting touches you'll make per channel.

Your touches should give you the highest probability of engaging prospects while reducing the chance that you become irritating spam or harm your brand reputation.

Examples:

- 5-4-3-2-1 = Phone 5×, Email 4×, Social 3×, In-person 2×, Video Message 1×
- 4-3-2-1 = Phone 4×, Email 3×, LinkedIn 2×, Video Message 1×
- 3-3-3-1 = Phone 3×, Email 3×, Social 3×, Snail Mail 1×

The combinations, duration, and touches are endless and there is no one-size-fits-all-lists solution. Therefore, you'll need to A/B test until you find the right combination for your targeted lists. This is where AI can really help you by analyzing what is working and helping you optimize your sequences.

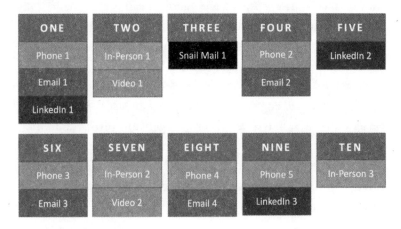

ONE	TWO	THREE	FOUR	FIVE
Phone 1	In-Person 1	Snail Mail 1	Phone 2	LinkedIn 2
Email 1	Video 1		Email 2	
LinkedIn 1				

SIX	SEVEN	EIGHT	NINE	TEN
Phone 3	In-Person 2	Phone 4	Phone 5	In-Person 3
Email 3	Video 2	Email 4	LinkedIn 3	

Duration and Spacing

Duration is the length of time over which your sequence of touches will run: 10 days, 15 days, 30 days, 60 days, 90 days, and so on.

While planning duration, account for the proximity of future buying windows, the size of the accounts on your targeted list, and the objective of the sequencing campaign. Typically, sequences targeting large accounts with hard-to-engage stakeholders will have a longer duration than sequences targeting smaller prospects with shorter sales cycles.

Optimize the spacing intervals between your prospecting touches within your cadence: daily, every other day, once a week, on certain days of the week, and so on. For each prospecting channel, you'll need to test the days of the week and time of day that convert best for your targeted list. For example, you may find that mornings work best for telephone prospecting touches while lunchtime works best for social media touches.

There are dozens of studies on the best times of day and week for prospecting touches. In aggregate, though, these studies are inconclusive at best. Your best bet is to continuously try different spacing for your touches and leverage AI to analyze what works best for you in your industry.

AI-Driven Prospecting Sequence Design

Crafting an effective multitouch sequence is an art and a science. It can be complicated. You need to leverage both data and your human intuition to get it right. Up until now the only way to do this was through manual A/B testing. But because this type of testing can be time consuming and overwhelming, most salespeople never do it.

AI can be a game changer for designing prospecting sequences because it can crunch and analyze historical data to identify patterns that lead to successful conversions way faster than you can. It can suggest the optimal number of touches, the best channels, and the ideal cadence, duration, and spacing between each interaction.

Of course, AI is fallible, so you need to apply human intelligence and intuition to check your robot and optimize your sequences. It's also crucial to understand that this data-driven approach only works if there is good data (remember the Robot Rules). This means you must run lots of experimental sequences in different iterations before your AI can do its best work.

Understanding the effectiveness of your multitouch sequences is crucial for continuous improvement. AI provides deep insights and analytics, tracking metrics like open rates, response rates, and conversion rates. This data is invaluable for refining your sequences, ensuring they become more effective over time.

EXERCISE 26.1: AI FOR PROSPECTING SEQUENCES

Consider all the AI tools, features, and plug-ins that are built into your current sales tech stack as well as those that are outside of your tech stack and how these tools can be applied to help you run better prospecting sequences.

AI Application	How/Why/When You Use It to Build and Manage Prospecting Sequences

27

Targeted Lists

*I*t is a fact that the better your list, the better your prospecting *outcomes. Therefore, effective prospecting sequences begin and end with targeted lists.*

Selling as a profession in the United States is roughly 125 years old. For this entire span, sales professionals of every generation have constantly asked, "Whom should I call?" And after 125 years, we are still terrible at building good prospecting lists. For this reason, the most promising AI transformation in sales will be building better and more targeted prospecting lists.

The Future of List Building: Right Prospect Plus Right Time

Imagine how things would change for you if, as you started your sales day, your company's sales AI handed you a targeted list of highly qualified prospects that are in the buying window. It would be revolutionary because suddenly your prospecting energy, touches, and conversations would be focused solely on engaging prospects that were making buying decisions.

There will be a day in which AI will analyze your current customer base to determine your ideal customer profile (ICP). Then by analyzing a set of disparate information, including intent data, your CRM, social media, website visitors, and anticipated buying windows and behavior, it will rapidly generate lists of prospects that are most likely to engage, move into your pipeline, and buy.

Sadly, this holy grail doesn't exist just yet. Because this AI application is insanely complex and must be built for each unique company, we are unlikely to see a working version of this that *actually works* very soon. The good news is that, as we wait, AI can jump in and help you with developing better lists now.

Define Your ICP

Yogi Berra once quipped, "If you don't know where you're going, you might end up somewhere else." This is apt advice for qualifying. If you don't know what qualified looks like, then you'll probably end up doing a lot of praying, and the Gods of Sales answering your prayer with "No!"

Therefore, the first step toward more effective qualifying is developing an ideal customer profile (ICP). This profile is a composite that may include qualification points, such as:

- Company size
- Estimated spend
- Industry vertical
- Growth trajectory
- Financial and creditworthiness
- Number of employees, locations, customers, physical assets

- Cap Ex budget
- Use cases for your product, software, solution
- Stakeholder hierarchies
- Competitor entrenchment
- Buying motivations, intent, and trigger events
- Problems
- Fit for your company
- And more

Analyzing all of this is not easy for humans. But it's a walk in the park for robots. AI can quickly analyze your database for patterns and commonalities among your best customers, uncover the stakeholder roles most likely to be involved in decision-making based on past sales data, analyze the deals you are closing, and gain a deeper understanding of trigger events that opened those buying windows.

AI can also segment the prospects in your CRM based on ICP data to ensure that you are focused on the highest potential opportunities and enable you to tailor your sequences and develop relevant messaging for specific segments.

Though this level of analysis and data crunching is more likely to be executed at an enterprise level by a marketing team rather than individual sellers, it can and will help you target the right prospects.

Intent

The easiest way to sell more is to spend 100% of your time talking with prospects who are in open buying windows and ready to buy. AI is already making this possible by analyzing and scoring leads based on intent data.

In the 21st century we leave behavioral breadcrumbs everywhere we go—what we search for online, what sites we visit, content we download, videos we watch, articles we read, what we purchase, emails we open, and social media activity, among many other signals. Some of this data about prospects comes from their interactions with you and your company online. Some is collected from external sources, third-party data providers, and broader market and industry trends.

When this collection of behavioral signals is analyzed along with other data, it can help zero in on and target buyers who have a high level of intent to purchase a product, software, or service. By leveraging intent data, you can prioritize leads and engage with prospects at the right time with the right messaging, improving prospecting conversion rates and ultimately increasing closing ratios.

It is likely that, if you have access to these types of data tools, you have already been exposed to intent data and scoring. You may have already or will soon begin seeing this in your CRM. AI is already processing vast amounts of intent data from both first-party and third-party sources to help salespeople identify prospects most likely to buy. Data providers like ZoomInfo are hard at work training their AIs and perfecting intent models. It will only get better.

This timely insight ensures that you reach out to prospects at the moment they are most receptive to your message, but only if you understand it and use it. While some of the opportunities for AI to transform sales are moonshots at the moment, intent data is reality now. Though it is far from perfect, now is the time to start familiarizing yourself with intent data and learning how to use it while it is in its nascent stages.

Prioritizing Lead Follow-up with Predictive Lead Scoring

We've already established that salespeople, in general, hate outbound prospecting. Most would rather have a steady stream of inbound leads. And though it is almost impossible for any organization to keep its sales team completely fed with inbound leads, the goal of most marketing teams is to produce as many as they can.

But there is one major problem. Though this bounty of inbound leads is supposed to be warmer than cold outreach, most are no warmer than your coldest cold call. When you complain about these leads, you hurt your marketing team's feelings, because they believe that every lead is a lead worth pursuing. This, of course leads to the age-old argument between marketing and sales, with sales crying that the "leads are weak" and marketing shooting back, "No, *you* are weak."

AI's predictive lead-scoring capabilities help prioritize prospects based on their likelihood to convert, allowing salespeople to focus their efforts where they're most likely to pay off. This ensures that your multitouch sequences are not just well-crafted but also targeted at the prospects with the highest potential for success.

With intent data and AI-driven analysis, we may finally settle this conflict and move past the standard marketing-qualified lead (MQL) and sales-qualified lead (SQL) classifications and into an age in which inbound leads are scored, segmented, and prioritized based on intent.

Multithreading

Imagine walking into a party. You don't just talk to the first person you meet and call it a night. No, you mingle, you chat with multiple folks, sharing stories and making connections.

That's multithreaded prospecting in a nutshell. It's about not putting all your eggs in one basket, or in sales terms, not relying on a single contact within your target account. It's about having conversations with multiple stakeholders and getting high, wide, and deep within an account.

With complex B2B sales, decisions aren't made in isolation. You'll need to get beyond the traditional "decision-makers" to build a coalition of stakeholders to help you build the case for doing business with you.

This is why you must actively work to identify and talk with each person who has a "stake" in the outcome of the deal—diversifying your outreach across different contacts within an organization. You should leave nothing to chance.

By engaging multiple stakeholders, you improve deal win probability. The challenge is: Who? Whom do you reach out to? Who has a stake? Who is interested beyond those in a traditional decision-maker role?

Back to intent data. AI's ability to analyze disparate behavioral signals and attribute those signals to individual stakeholders within an organization is the key to putting multithreading outreach on steroids. This is where access to data platforms like ZoomInfo, Cognism, Apollo, Seamless, and LeadIQ really pays off—especially when these platforms are integrated with your CRM. With this information in hand, you can quickly tailor your messaging and sequences to individual stakeholders to grab their attention.

At the end of the day, sales is about people. It's about connections, relationships, and understanding. No amount of technology can replace the genuine rapport you build through real, human interaction. As you weave your multithreaded prospecting web, never lose sight of the person on the other end of each thread.

28

Message Matters

T he most difficult element of prospecting sequences is
crafting effective messages. The good news is that this is
an area where artificial intelligence plus human emotional
intelligence can make the job easier and message generation
much faster.

On its own, with a few prompts from you, AI is perfectly
capable of crafting prospecting messages. But as you learned in
Chapter 19, robots leave recognizable patterns. When people
know that a robot wrote your message, it will land cold.

It is also true that AI prospecting messages tend to lack
emotion and human authenticity. They are stiff, like a marketing
brochure. They do not resonate or grab your prospect's attention.
This figure shows a stiff prospecting message:

You must be very careful and intentional when plugging into AI to get help with crafting prospecting messaging. AI can speed you up, but to create authentic messaging that connects emotionally, that requires your human advantage and empathy.

In this chapter we'll explore the two types of prospecting messages: *personalized* and *targeted*.[1]

- **Personalized** messages are heavily researched messages, used in high-stakes situations and crafted for one specific person.

- **Targeted** messages are handy when you need to move fast in high-velocity situations, touching many prospects in

---

[1]Jeb Blount first discussed this in his book Virtual Selling: A Quick-Start Guide to Leveraging Video, Technology, and Virtual Communication Channels to Engage Remote Buyers and Close Deals Fast (Wiley, 2020).

a short period of time, when stopping to craft a separate personalized message for each prospect is not practical.

Personalized Prospecting Messages

When the stakes are high and you need to grab the attention of a high-level decision-maker, a personalized message is the way to go. In some cases, you may only get one shot to engage a C-level executive, so you need to be relevant and give them a compelling reason to agree to give you time. To break through, you must clearly demonstrate that you've done your homework and have taken the time to understand your prospect's unique situation.

Crafting personalized prospecting messages is time consuming. It requires research and a concerted effort to get the message right. For this reason, it makes sense to seek out help from AI.

Though AI can assist you with research and even insight, be cautioned that personalization at scale, done by AI, has major flaws.

- AI sometimes gets things wrong, leading to embarrassing, credibility-killing mistakes.
- Robot personalization, more often than not, is merely a shallow façade of personal facts scraped from the internet and social media platforms.
- AI loves to combine these personal tidbits with gratuitous, sometimes cringeworthy flattery, such as, "I'm really impressed with what you are doing over at XYZ company." Executives easily see right through this and know that you didn't put in the work.

Effective personalization should build up your credibility and authority, not damage it. Certainly, AI can speed up the process of research and gathering information when you are working on personalized messages. But this is one place where you, the human, must put your heart and intellect into crafting the perfect message.

Show Me You Know Me

The real secret to crafting personalized messages that reduce resistance and convert prospecting calls into meetings is remembering a simple but powerful premise: people make decisions based on emotion first, and then justify with logic. In other words, they feel, then they think.

This is why the way robots typically write prospecting messages doesn't work. AI pitches rely on rational arguments that focus on features and overlook emotion. This is especially true when the message is filled with easy-to-spot robot patterns.

Prospects abhor these messages. Instead, they want to feel that you get them and understand their problems (emotional and logical), or are at least trying to. Before they'll agree to give up their time to meet with you, they need to sense a human connection. From their perspective, it's "Show me you know me!" Everyone desires to be understood. Personalized prospecting messages should build a bridge from the problems your prospect is facing (their reasons) and how you might help them.

Understanding their reasons requires research, reading, and gaining insight from conversations with other people in their industry. You need to put in the work to get to know what they are dealing with and how your product, service, or software can help them.

- This requires you to check their social media profiles for what they are posting, liking, and sharing.
- Listen to podcast interviews.
- Read news and PR posts about them.

- Read articles they have written.
- Watch videos they are in or have created.
- Research past activity with your company in your CRM.
- Validate their job title.
- Set up Google alerts to have information about the company or individual sent directly to your inbox.
- Browse the company, division, and location through online searches, websites, and press releases.
- Check out their company pages on LinkedIn and Facebook.
- Review their company website.
- Research trends in their industry.
- Research public information like 10-Ks and transcripts of shareholder calls.
- Make notes about jargon, core values, awards, trigger events, initiatives, changes, and problems that you can solve.

A failure to demonstrate that you know the company and their industry will cause your contacts to wonder if you're going to be able to help them. One way to prevent this is to meet with the salespeople who have already won deals in the industry you are pursuing to learn about the unique challenges your prospects in that industry are facing.

Release the Bots

If this sounds like a lot, it is—unless you get your bots working for you. Here are a few ways to accomplish this:

- The AI that is built into modern search engines and your CRM can send back results at lightning speed.

- Tools like ChatGPT, Claude, Microsoft's Copilot, and Google's Gemini can quickly summarize websites, articles, reports, and transcripts of calls and interviews.

- AI built into LinkedIn can make it easier to glean insight about your prospect.

These are just three examples. There is so much more that AI can do to help you zero in on who your prospect is as a person and the challenges and problems they need help with. All you need to do is start practicing with and using the AI you already have at your disposal to do the heavy lifting. We'll practice this in Exercise 28.1.

Craft the Message

Now, with the information your AI returns, apply your human intelligence, empathy, and intuition to craft a relevant message that relates to their unique situation, and shows them that you know them. Focus on specific problems they are facing and bridge to how you can help them. Here is an example:

> Hi, Windsor, this is Jeb Blount from Sales Gravy. The reason I'm calling is to set an appointment with you. I read in *Fast Company* that you are adding another hundred sales reps. I've worked with companies like yours to reduce ramp-up time for new reps. At Xjam Software, for example, we cut ramp-up time for their new reps by 50 percent. While I don't know if our solution will be a fit in your unique situation, I've got some ideas and best practices I've seen work well for companies like yours and thought you might be interested in learning more about them. How about we get together for a short meeting on Thursday at 2:00?

In Exercise 28.2, you'll craft a personalized prospecting message for the prospect you researched in Exercise 28.1.

EXERCISE 28.1: RESEARCH FOR PERSONALIZED MESSAGING

For this exercise, choose a high-value prospect with whom you want to get time. Then, using the AI you have at your disposal, practice researching this person, their company, and their industry to find insights you might use to craft a personalized prospecting message. Your goal is to find five relevant pieces of information, listing them in this table.

Prospect Name:
1.
2.
3.
4.
5.

EXERCISE 28.2: CRAFT A PERSONALIZED PROSPECTING MESSAGE

Once you have the five pieces of relevant information, use them to craft a message that will resonate with your prospect. Highlight these insights to establish yourself as a valuable resource they'll want to meet with.

Prospect Name:

Targeted Messaging

When you have a large prospect base combined with high activity expectations, taking time to research each prospect and craft a unique prospecting message before every call makes no sense. It would completely bog you down.

Therefore, to be efficient, you need prospecting messages that may be used for multiple prospects—one to many rather than one to one. The key here is crafting messages that will resonate with most of the people on your targeted list.

Since it is unlikely that you'll have deep and detailed information about the specific issues, problems, or concerns of each individual prospect or even that the information is in your CRM, you'll need to do a little work to help you better understand their situation.

You'll need to infer the problems they may be facing based on economic trends and what other businesses or people in their role are experiencing in the same industry, geographical area, or market segment, or with a certain competitor's product. This is where AI can help you.

Start with segmenting your prospect database into large groups of similar prospects. Then prompt your AI to do the heavy lifting. Here's an example prompt that works well:

What are some of the challenges that owners of small and medium-sized _____ companies are facing in our current economic market?

This figure shows an exchange with ChatGPT about business challenges:

You

What are some of the challenges that owners of small and medium sized staffing companies facing in our current economic market?

ChatGPT

Owners of small and medium-sized staffing companies are navigating a complex set of challenges in the current economic market. These challenges can vary widely depending on the region, industry sectors they serve, and the overall economic climate. However, some common issues they might be facing include:

1. **Talent Acquisition and Retention**: Finding and retaining skilled employees is a significant challenge, especially in competitive job markets. Staffing companies need to constantly adapt their recruitment strategies to attract top talent and develop retention programs to keep them.
2. **Regulatory Compliance**: Staying compliant with labor laws, tax regulations, and industry-specific standards can be particularly burdensome for small and medium-sized businesses that may not have dedicated legal or compliance teams.
3. **Cash Flow Management**: Staffing companies often face cash flow challenges due to the nature of their business model, which involves paying employees or contractors before receiving payment from clients. This can be exacerbated in uncertain economic times when clients may delay payments.
4. **Technological Adaptation**: Keeping up with technological advancements and integrating new systems into their operations can be both a challenge and an opportunity. Small and medium-sized staffing companies need to invest in technology to improve efficiency and service quality but may lack the resources or expertise to do so effectively.
5. **Market Competition**: Intense competition from both local and large multinational staffing firms can put pressure on smaller companies. Differentiating their services and demonstrating value to potential clients is crucial.
6. **Economic Uncertainty**: Fluctuations in the economy, such as recessions, can lead to reduced demand for staffing services as companies cut back on hiring. Economic uncertainty can also lead to volatility in various industry sectors that staffing companies serve.
7. **Client Diversification**: Relying on a limited number of clients or industries can be risky, especially if those sectors are hit hard by economic downturns. Diversifying their client base can help mitigate this risk but requires broadening their expertise and possibly expanding their service offerings.
8. **Pricing Pressure**: Balancing competitive pricing with maintaining healthy margins is a constant challenge. Price sensitivity among clients can lead to a race to the bottom, impacting profitability.

Addressing these challenges requires strategic planning, flexibility, and often, the adoption of new technologies or business models to improve operational efficiency, enhance client and candidate experiences, and ensure financial stability.

Here are some additional prompt examples:

- What are three major trends that are impacting businesses in the _____ industry?
- What are executives in _____ doing to cope with the _____ trend?
- What are the five biggest problems on the minds of owners of _____?

These prompts work because they are specific and targeted. AI can clearly understand what kind of information you want and present it clearly. You want to use open-ended questions, but you also need to be sure your wording is concrete and focused so you get responses that will help you.

Focus on Emotions

The most effective prospecting messages relate to your prospects' emotions like stress, worry, insecurity, distrust, anxiety, fear, frustration, and anger, or they offer them peace of mind, security, options, lower stress, less worry, or hope.

With the information you have gathered about their situation, use your human advantage and empathy to stand in their shoes and sense how their problems and challenges impact their emotions. Consider what they might be going through and how you might feel in their situation.

- What would cause you stress?
- What makes you worry?
- What creates the feeling of anxiety?
- What gives you peace of mind?

Use the answers to these questions to build messaging that is about your prospect rather than you. For example: "Because so many business owners in your position are stressed out over remaining compliant with the new payroll rules, we've developed a software system that eliminates mistakes that lead to fines."

A simple follow-on AI prompt like "How do these challenges impact their emotions?" can give you reference points on which to focus your empathy. See how this looks in the next figure:

 You
How do these challenges impact their emotions?

 ChatGPT
The challenges faced by owners of small and medium-sized staffing companies can significantly impact their emotions and mental well-being. Here's how these challenges might translate into emotional experiences:

1. **Stress and Anxiety**: Managing the day-to-day operations while navigating financial uncertainties, regulatory changes, and competitive pressures can lead to high levels of stress and anxiety. Concerns about cash flow, client retention, and talent acquisition can be particularly stressful.
2. **Overwhelm**: The need to wear multiple hats and handle various aspects of the business, from sales and marketing to compliance and employee management, can lead to feelings of overwhelm. This is especially true when resources are limited, and the business owner must juggle numerous tasks simultaneously.
3. **Frustration**: Dealing with the complexities of regulatory compliance, technological changes, and client demands can be frustrating. This frustration can be compounded when efforts to grow the business or improve efficiency are met with obstacles or slow progress.
4. **Uncertainty and Fear**: Economic fluctuations and market instability can create a sense of uncertainty and fear about the future of the business. Concerns about potential downturns, losing key clients, or not being able to meet payroll can be particularly fear-inducing.
5. **Isolation**: Business owners might feel isolated, especially if they lack a support network of peers or mentors who understand the unique challenges of the staffing industry. This isolation can be exacerbated when dealing with difficult issues that seem insurmountable.
6. **Pride and Satisfaction**: On the positive side, overcoming challenges and achieving business milestones can lead to feelings of pride and satisfaction. Successfully navigating a difficult economic landscape or securing a new client can be incredibly rewarding.
7. **Hope and Optimism**: Despite the challenges, the potential for growth and success can foster a sense of hope and optimism. Innovations in technology, new market opportunities, and successful client engagements can inspire confidence in the future.
8. **Burnout**: Prolonged exposure to high stress, constant problem-solving, and the pressure to perform can lead to burnout. This emotional exhaustion can impact the owner's ability to lead effectively and make sound business decisions.

Understanding these emotional impacts is crucial for developing strategies to support business owners, whether through offering solutions that alleviate some of their burdens, providing platforms for community and support, or helping them find ways to manage stress and maintain a healthy work-life balance.

Craft Targeted Messages

Build several targeted prospecting messages for each segment of prospects or targeted list. Test and refine them. As you engage in conversations with these prospects, you'll naturally iterate and refine your message Here is an example:

> Hi, Candace, this is Jeb Blount from Sales Gravy. The reason I'm calling is to grab a few minutes on your calendar, because I find that so many leaders like you are frustrated with how long it takes to get new salespeople ramped up to full productivity. Our powerful AI-assisted digital sales training platform has been proven to cut onboarding time in half for new sales reps and get them selling fast. How about we get together for a short meeting so I can learn more about you and see whether it makes sense to schedule a demo? I have 2:00 p.m. on Thursday available.

You'll notice that I implied that Candace is frustrated that it is taking too long to get her new salespeople up to speed and selling. I don't know for sure that this is her issue, but because most companies that are hiring salespeople have this problem, there is a good chance she has this problem, too.

Remember that targeted prospecting messages are like horseshoes and hand grenades—they don't need to be perfect, just good enough to convert your prospecting calls into an appointment, conversation, or qualifying information.

Stop now and, using Exercise 28.3, practice crafting targeted prospecting messages for each of your major prospect types, roles, industries, or segments.

EXERCISE 28.3: CRAFT TARGETED PROSPECTING MESSAGES

Pull together everything you've learned to create a targeted prospecting message for different segments in your industry. Mention an emotion you suspect your prospect is experiencing due to a challenge they're facing.

Segment	Targeted Prospecting Message

29

Slow Prospecting

My *new client smiled as I finished walking him through my final presentation. He said, "I love everything you showed me and feel confident that this is the solution we need to achieve our growth goals this year. What blows my mind is how this all came together.*

"I've been following your content on LinkedIn for several years. Then, when I was looking for help with my sales team, I sent your LinkedIn profile to my executive assistant to contact you and here we are ten days later doing business!"

For my part, I had no idea that this company even existed. It was never on my radar. Yet there it was, suddenly in my pipeline because of the slow prospecting work I had been doing on LinkedIn each morning for years.

For most of this section we've been focused on fast prospecting—interrupt, engage, ask for time. Slow prospecting is different. It is nuanced and strategic. It's playing the long game.

It is the process of personal branding, creating familiarity, shaping opinions, creating awareness, and nurturing high-value targets until the time is right. It's about setting the conditions that cause opportunities to knock on your door.

Social Selling Is Hard Work

Slow prospecting techniques include developing a professional network, networking and community engagement, nurturing high-value prospects, and most importantly for modern sellers, social selling activity on platforms like LinkedIn.

LinkedIn has profoundly impacted the ability of B2B sales professionals to connect with prospects. Similarly, Facebook, Instagram, YouTube, X, and TikTok are integral to successful B2C and B2B sales approaches. The social channel, used effectively, enhances, elevates, and sometimes accelerates your fast prospecting efforts.

When you are running fast and slow at the same time, you can make a lot of money. What cannot be discounted, though, is that slow prospecting is hard work and takes a long time. There is very little instant gratification. Where the feedback loop on fast prospecting is almost instant, slow prospecting is about faith that, by doing the right things consistently over the long haul, you'll get a return on your investment.

This is, of course, why the majority of salespeople fail at slow prospecting. They never stick with it long enough for the magic to happen. The primary reason that they quit is that social media is freaking hard work. The grind is real and can be exhausting. There are days when you'll be sick of it. Getting value from and adding value to the social channel requires consistent, focused, and regimented discipline.

To be effective with social media, you must be active every single day. Consistency is crucial. A post here and a like there, randomly and infrequently, is like tossing a small pebble into the ocean and expecting it to generate a wave.

A big challenge is breaking through the ocean of content flooding social media platforms. This makes it difficult to stand out and get noticed. Social media platform algorithms—the hidden programs that determine whether or not your posts get seen—reward consistency. The more consistent your activity, the higher the probability that your posts get moved to the top of feeds, earning you more eyeballs.

The Law of Familiarity

Think of your favorite actor. You know their face, vocal patterns, body language, and mannerisms. You are drawn to the movies and TV shows they star in. There is a comfort level with them that causes you to enjoy seeing them in almost any role.

If you saw them in public, you'd recognize them instantly. You'd be starstruck and feel compelled to walk up and express how big a fan you are or tell them about the impact they've had on your life. You'd be excited to ask for a selfie or get an autograph.

But, if you think back, it wasn't always like this. You didn't feel this level of connection the very first time you saw them on screen. You became a fan over time, after seeing them many times. The more familiar they became to you, the more you liked them. At some point, they crossed your familiarity threshold. Only then did you put them on a pedestal and become a fan.

With social media, the name of the game is *familiarity*. Familiarity leads to liking. The more familiar a prospect is with you, the more likely they will be to engage. Familiarity is sales lubrication. It takes the friction out of cold calling and building relationships. It makes everything easier. The lack of familiarity is why you get so many objections. When people don't know you, it's much harder for them to trust you.

Never in the human experience has it been easier for individuals to build familiarity. Point, shoot, write, click, and post—it's all at your fingertips. You can get your name and reputation out there fast and for very little cost. AI makes this process even easier.

To build familiarity, you must make a direct investment in improving the awareness of your name, expertise, and reputation. You must be present and consistently engaging on social media so that people see you often and, over time, become more comfortable with you.

Engaging means posting valuable content along with liking, sharing, and commenting on the posts of your targeted prospects and account stakeholders. In time, just as you did with your favorite actor, your targeted prospects will cross the familiarity threshold with you. When stakeholders begin to feel like they know you, doors open and setting meetings becomes easier.

In *Eat Their Lunch,* Anthony wrote about the long game. He makes a list of 60 large prospects and reaches out to three each day. This strategy will have you communicating to every large client at least once a month, building familiarity and keeping you top of mind.

The Authority Principle

We seek the guidance of experts because it makes it easier to navigate uncertainty and make faster decisions in a complex world. This is called the authority principle—sharing and publishing relevant and valuable content (on LinkedIn and other social media outlets) that is intriguing to prospects and helps them solve problems and positions you as an expert.

When you confidently project yourself as a subject matter expert in your field, it draws prospects to you like a magnet and entices them to engage. As they engage, you gain insight into the problems they are facing, opportunities to help them, and influence over their buying decisions.

Intuitively, we know that salespeople who can educate, offer insight, and solve problems are far more valuable than those whose primary sales strategy is to pitch products and services. Therefore, you will engage more prospects and sell more to them when you are valuable.

In the social channel, the primary way you provide value is through content that educates, builds credibility, anchors familiarity, and positions you as an expert who can solve relevant problems. The right content shared at the right time with the right prospects creates connections and converts passive online relationships into real-time conversations.

Content Creation

Creating and publishing original content is the most powerful way to build your personal brand and helps burnish your reputation as an expert in your field. Original content is also more likely to pull in comments and be shared.

Social media algorithms place greater emphasis on original content—especially content that is posted natively. This means that your post isn't linked to an original article or video on another website. The most effective forms of original content that are the easiest for sales professionals to create and post include the types of media detailed in the following sections.

Video

Video consumption is voracious and growing. It's easy to shoot and upload original videos; just press record on your phone and start talking. Some ideas include:

- Short videos of you expounding on a relevant subject
- Behind the scenes at your office or place of work
- Product delivery or installation at a customer account
- Customer testimonials
- Clips from webinars
- Interviews with subject matter experts

One of the most effective ways to use videos is to break long videos into many small videos. A new generation of AI tools like Opus.pro and Descript make this process infinitely easier.

You'll also find powerful AI video editing tools built into platforms like Vimeo and mobile apps like Videoleap.

Likewise, there are dozens of video creation tools like Pictory that allow you to create AI-generated video from text.

Pictures and Infographics

Images are the fastest and easiest way to add original content to your social media channels. Ideas include:

- Fun pictures of you and your colleagues on the job
- Company events and charitable work
- You receiving an award
- You with your customers, new products, or behind the scenes
- Trend infographics
- Data infographics
- Process infographics
- How-to infographics

Image-based AI tools are being built into many creative platforms these days. One of our absolute favorites for developing social media posts is Canva with its wide array of templates, infographics, and increasingly sophisticated AI integrations. And, of course, there is Dall-E, the AI image generator that started it all.

Articles

LinkedIn allows you to post full-length original articles. These articles may include images, videos, and links to other resources (good for lead gen).

AI can help you write relevant articles faster. Be warned, though, that the social channels are getting wise to purely AI-generated content and consider this type of content spam. As you learned in Part 4, it is essential that you add your human touch and originality to anything AI helps you write and never forget Robot Rule One.

Long-Form Posts

An easy way to create more posts from original articles is to pull excerpts from them to use for long-form posts. These are two- to three-paragraph single-topic posts of 175 words or less. AI can do this for you in a jiffy. Just paste your article into ChatGPT, Claude, or Gemini and prompt it to give you 175-word summaries.

Short-Form Posts

Short posts of 280 characters or less can garner a lot of attention when you have the right content. AI can quickly repurpose long-form content into short posts. Just paste an article, transcript, or media file into your AI assistant and prompt: *Please give me five short social media posts from this content.* In a matter of seconds you'll be in business.

Content Curation

The social channel is a voracious and insatiable beast that devours content. It must be fed daily for you and your message to remain relevant and present. You'll never be able to create enough original content to keep up.

The solution to this problem is curation. A simple analogy for curation is the act of clipping articles from magazines and newspapers and sending them to someone. Except that on social media, you are doing this digitally and amplifying the impact by going from a one-to-one analog footprint to one-to-many digital distribution.

Instead of publishing your own original content, you leverage the content that is being created and published by others. Essentially, you become a maven who aggregates the most relevant content for your audience and shares it through your various social media newsfeeds.

The beautiful thing about content curation is that even though you didn't produce the content, some of the credit for the content rubs off on you. There are three pillars of an effective social media content curation strategy:

- Awareness
- Sources
- Intent

Awareness

You need to be aware of what is happening in your industry—trends, competitors, and movers and shakers. Have your eyes and ears open, pay attention to what is going on around you, and consume industry-specific blogs, webinars, and videos.

AI assistants can help with this research and keep relevant information in front of you. Use simple prompts to gain insight on industry trends and automation to get new information sent to you.

Sources

You'll need good sources for content. Pull from your company blog, podcast, and YouTube channel. Leverage industry blogs and trade publications. Tap into the thought leaders who are shaping the dialog in your industry. Grab relevant articles from news sources like the *Wall Street Journal*. Use your company's library of content.

AI is brilliant at both helping you find relevant sources and summarizing articles, videos, podcasts, and transcripts. This allows you to review and consume more sources and information faster.

Intent

Rather than just randomly and disparately sharing, be intentional about your content strategy. Take time to read and understand what you are sharing, so that you may include insightful comments with the content you share. AI can even help you craft these comments and takeaways.

An Explosion of AI-Powered Social Media Tools

The good news is that there is an explosion of new AI-powered tools that can make it much easier to keep your social media presence consistent and strong. Many AI-powered social media tools will even rate and score the content you are sharing for relevance and the potential to go viral. This can help you make better decisions about the content that you choose to post and share.

We've named a few of these tools in this chapter but there are far more out there than we can possibly list in the pages of this book. Take a moment now to do an online search, or better yet, ask your AI assistant to help you discover tools that can elevate your slow prospecting activities to the next level.

PART 6

Qualifying, Pre-call Planning, Discovery

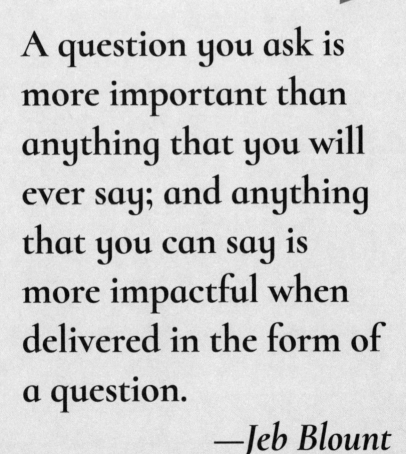

A question you ask is more important than anything that you will ever say; and anything that you can say is more impactful when delivered in the form of a question.

—*Jeb Blount*

30

Everything in Sales Begins with a Qualified Opportunity

*L*osing *a deal because you failed to qualify it properly is excruci-atingly painful. We've all been there, working our asses off on a deal only to find out after all of the work has been done that:*

- We're dealing with the wrong person or people.
- The stakeholders have no commitment to change.
- There is no budget.
- The account is still under contract with a competitor.
- The buying window has closed or has not opened.
- The company has no credit.
- The prospect's organization is the wrong fit for your application, solutions, software, product, service, or company culture.

The list of disqualifiers that kill deals goes on but you get the drift. It is here, on these rocks, that unwary and undisciplined salespeople crash and burn—sometimes with career-ending results.

The brutal truth is that in sales, nothing matters if you are not dealing with a qualified opportunity. You can be the greatest sales pro ever to walk the face of the earth and an absolute master of AI, but if you are wasting your time with an unqualified prospect, you will fail. Period. End of story.

Effective qualifying requires a systematic and methodical focus on turning the unknowns into the known. It can be tedious and time consuming, which is why salespeople shortcut or ignore qualifying, leaving their fate to chance.

And let's keep it real—sometimes you don't want to know the truth. Because the truth is that "dream account" in your pipeline, the one you're projecting to close this quarter, is actually a delusional nightmare that will never buy and is sucking the life out of you.

Qualified prospects and stakeholders are scarce, and a moment spent with a low-probability prospect takes you away from your most important task—investing in prospects who will buy.

Developing an Ideal Customer Profile

Qualifying activity happens into two primary buckets:

1. Before you put a prospect into your pipeline

2. During the sales process once a prospect is in your pipeline

AI is particularly effective at gathering factual information to help you qualify and target the right prospects before you put them into your pipeline. It can comb through reams of information to uncover the qualifying points that are most important to you, then analyze this information against intent data to help you score and target the right prospects.

Effective qualifying begins with defining your ideal customer profile (ICP). This profile is a composite that includes the buying window, compelling buying motivations, stakeholder hierarchies, stakeholder engagement, competitor entrenchment, sales cycle, industry vertical, company size, and fit, among other attributes.

An ICP helps you target, nurture, and engage the right prospects at the right time. Leverage the ICP to build targeted prospecting lists and benchmark existing pipeline opportunities.

Artificial intelligence is a game changer for ICP development. AI can analyze your company's internal data to find patterns and commonalities among your best and most profitable customers.

Your AI can also analyze the deals your sales team are closing to gain a deeper understanding of the events that trigger the opening of buying windows along with the common stakeholder roles that are responsible for purchasing what you sell. This data will help you develop a profile of the prospects most likely to do business with you and, over the long term, be profitable, happy customers.

Leveraging Human Intelligence and Intuition

Of course, not every prospect will fit your ICP profile perfectly. This is not how the real world works. Most opportunities are imperfect.

Qualification is a combination of both data and human intuition. You must consider factual evidence and listen to your gut instinct when assessing the viability of an opportunity.

Once a prospect enters your pipeline and you begin conducting discovery conversations with stakeholders, you must maintain acute awareness for signs that might disqualify or lower the win probability of your deal along with signals that you need to go all in with a particular prospect. Your human advantage is asking artful and strategic questions during discovery conversations: assessing stakeholder engagement, testing assumptions, putting AI-surfaced data into context, and sensing nuance.

In the near future, however, the AI integrated into your CRM should be able to use the information you (and other members of your team) enter following meetings with stakeholders along with other intent, engagement, competitor, and closed won or lost data to dynamically qualify and assign win probability scores.

A Lethal Qualifying Machine

No matter your chosen qualifying methodology—BANT, MEDDIC, PACT, TAS, or WOLFE—integrating AI into your qualifying process will help you make better decisions with where you invest your time and effort, improve the accuracy of your forecasts, and increase your closing ratio.

- AI can research and surface qualifying data points at lightning speed.
- You can see humancentric disqualifiers like lack of engagement, an attachment to an incumbent vendor, or motivation to change that AI cannot.
- AI can monitor disparate information streams over the course of the sales process and alert you to warning signals that your deal may be in jeopardy or that there is a need for a course correction.
- You know when to take an educated risk in imperfect situations based on intuition, nuance, and context.
- AI brings clarity to emotions—especially attachment—that can cloud your judgment.

When you put AI and human intelligence together, it makes you an especially lethal qualifying machine.

31

The Art of Discovery

D *iscovery is the most important step in the sales process. It is*
the key to building the case for doing business with you and
closing the deal. It is where 80 percent or more of your time should
be spent, and where relationships with stakeholders are developed
and anchored. Discovery is where you earn your stripes as a sales
professional.

The psychology of discovery is complicated. Your stakeholders
are concerned about whether you are only there for their money,
or if you can genuinely help them. You, on the other hand, are
first attempting to ascertain if they are truly qualified and second
to gather the information that you need to help them.

If you believe selling is difficult, try being a decision-maker.
No matter a person's role or title, no one wants to be responsible
for a mistake that makes a problem even worse. You can live
through a lost deal, but stakeholders may find it difficult to
recover from buying mistakes and their status downgraded inside

their company. Spreading this risk to other people is one of the key reasons why so many people are involved in buying decisions these days.

Depending on the complexity of the deal, discovery may last a few minutes or span many months and require meetings with a broad array of stakeholders. During discovery, you must be patient and methodical. The objective is to leverage strategic, artful, and provocative questions to:

- Evoke awareness in stakeholders about the need to change.
- Challenge the status quo and shake stakeholders from their comfort zones.
- Demonstrate your sincere desire to help them.
- Eliminate or neutralize perceived alternatives to doing business with you.

Except for qualifying and putting the right deals into the pipeline in the first place, nothing else in the sales process has a greater impact on your ability to close the sale than conducting effective discovery conversations.

Discovery Is Human

The art of discovery is a uniquely human endeavor. It requires intention, strategy, and planning. You must ask open-ended questions, demonstrate sincere interest, use your empathy, and listen. AI cannot do this job for you.

Discovery isn't sexy. It can be slow, time-consuming, and emotionally challenging. It's so much easier to run quickly through a handful of self-serving, closed-ended questions, email over a proposal, and hope for the best than it is to take the time to truly understand what is important to your prospect and their stakeholders. But when human-to-human interaction gets replaced with shortcuts and arm's-length communication, failure isn't far behind. One of the primary reasons so many salespeople struggle to close sales and make their number is that their discovery is weak and inadequate.

Consider Rachel, an account executive, who walks into the office of a new prospect, introduces herself, and begins pitching her company and products.

Ted, the buyer, eventually tires of the pitch and cuts her off with "Rachel, our current vendor is doing a pretty good job right now, but we are always open to other quotes. Here is a spec sheet of what we're using now. Work something up, send it to me, and then we can talk. I just want you to know, though, that you'll need to get your prices right."

Rachel dashes back to her office and puts information into her AI-powered proposal platform. It quickly spits out a quote, which she emails to Ted. Then she puts the opportunity into her forecast.

During her Monday morning one-to-one, she tells her sales manager about the opportunity. "I'm talking to the decision-maker, and he's super-interested! I'm positive that I'll close it."

Three days later, Rachel calls Ted on the phone. "Ted, I'm just checking in about my quote."

"Your prices are much higher than what we're paying now," he responds.

Rachel pitches, "We gave you our most aggressive pricing. But our product is much higher quality than what you're getting now, and it has more features."

"That may be true, but what we're using now is working. Besides, it can't be that different. You're all about the same. We're going to stick with our current vendor."

Because there was no discovery, Rachel has no relationship, no context, no information, and no basis on which to explain the value she's offering. As far as Ted is concerned, there is no difference between her product and her competitors' other than price.

Sound familiar? For many salespeople, this is a normal day. AI cannot close this gap for you. Discovery conversations, conducted effectively, are uniquely human.

The Problem with Icebergs

If you've ever had a chance to see an iceberg up close, you know how impressively huge they can be. What is hard to fathom, though, is that what you see is only a small portion of the total mass, most of which is hidden below the water's surface.

Stakeholders are much like icebergs. They reveal only surface information, while keeping their real problems and emotions hidden from view. It is not natural for stakeholders to allow sellers to look below the surface. By keeping certain things concealed, buyers attempt to protect themselves and strengthen their power position.

Discovery is a language of questions. To get below the surface, you will need to ask artfully structured questions in the context of a fluid conversation. When you treat discovery as a fluid conversation, you disarm your stakeholders, draw them in, lower their emotional walls, get beneath the surface, and gather the information you need to build an unassailable case for doing business with you.

The more you show genuine interest in what your stakeholders are saying, the more valuable and important they feel. The better they feel, the more they will want to talk. The more they talk, the more connected they will feel to you. As you connect, you gain the right to ask the deeper, more probing questions that get below the surface to the real information you need.

Artful questions are provocative. Sometimes they are just simple statements with a pause that elicit responses to fill in the silence. They cause the stakeholder to think and become self-aware. Artful questions naturally build on the conversation rather than running parallel—and separately—from it. They must match the moment. Empathy, situational awareness, attention control, emotional control, and confidence are necessary to create artful questions that match the moment.

Many deals are won during discovery because a well-placed question creates doubt about potential alternatives: the current vendor, a competitor, another system or process, the belief that it can be done in-house, or doing nothing. Artful questions encourage stakeholders to consider the implications and risks of failing to act. It is here that the decision to select you and your company as the vendor of choice begins to form.

Conducting discovery conversations is what you are uniquely designed to do as a human. It is what you do best. But effective discovery doesn't just happen. It requires planning and preparation, and this is where AI can be a powerful force. In a moment we'll jump into pre-discovery call planning, but first let's look at the biggest mistakes to avoid with discovery.

32

Eight Big Discovery Mistakes You Need to Avoid

T here are a distinct set of mistakes sales professionals tend to make when it comes to discovery conversations. These mistakes have nothing to do with AI and everything to do with human fallacy and lack of discipline.

AI cannot help you avoid these mistakes. This responsibility rests squarely on your shoulders. Here is a short list of what you need to avoid.

Taking Shortcuts

The majority of the mistakes with discovery happen because salespeople don't understand the value of discovery. When you don't value discovery you take shortcuts. You invest 10% of your time in discovery rather than 80%. You go through the motions, check the boxes, and fail to listen. This leads to shallow discovery, a weak business case, broken relationships, and a much lower closing ratio.

Asking Stupid Questions

When you ask your stakeholders questions that you should already know the answers to, you are exhibiting your lack of preparation and commitment. For example, stupid question number one is "What do you do here?" (One of my young sellers asked this question. His prospect groaned. We were in and out of the meeting in five minutes. #truestory)

If you can easily find a piece of information on the internet or social media, you should not ask about it in a discovery meeting. The most effective questions position you as an expert consultant by demonstrating that you understand your prospect's business, industry, challenges, and opportunities.

Self-Orientation

Too many salespeople focus on their outcomes instead of those of their prospect. Stakeholders don't meet with you to help you hit your quota. They are there to solve their own problems. When discovery conversations are all about you—transactional rather than relational—it kills opportunities. Stakeholders don't want to be transacted. They don't want to waste any additional time answering your self-serving, leading questions. There is no value for them, so they move on and end up ghosting you.

Focusing on Your Next Question Rather Than Listening

One of the biggest mistakes that salespeople make during discovery conversations is getting so wrapped up in the process of asking the next question that they stop listening to the answer to the one they just asked.

When you are not listening, stakeholders know it, especially when they have to repeat themselves because you were not paying attention. The failure to listen destroys relationships fast.

When you disconnect from the conversation because you are thinking about your next question, it causes the discovery conversation to feel disjointed and forced. Rather than asking one question after another from a predetermined list, choose a conversational, organic approach where each question builds on the last, based on your stakeholder's answers.

Interrogation versus Conversation

Imagine a scene from a movie. The villain is strapped to a chair in the middle of an empty room. A bright light is pointed into his eyes while the interrogator peppers him with accusatory, leading, closed-ended questions. The interrogator intends to make the villain feel as uncomfortable as possible and push him off-balance, breaking him down so that in a moment of weakness he reveals his deepest secrets.

Many salespeople put their prospects in a similarly uncomfortable position. These salespeople unload an avalanche of closed-ended, leading questions that may come off as imposing, self-serving, and manipulative. In response, prospects deflect, obfuscate, and erect emotional barriers.

By contrast, artfully structured, open-ended questions asked in the context of a fluid conversation keep stakeholders engaged. When you treat discovery as a fluid conversation rather than an interrogation, you disarm your stakeholders, draw them in, and lower emotional walls.

Asking Hard Questions First

Imagine that you see a stranger from a distance, someone you don't know, walking in your direction, making a beeline right toward you. As they come to a halt in front of you, your guard is up. Then, without hesitation, they begin peppering you with personal questions:

- Where do you live?
- What's your mom's maiden name?
- How many kids do you have? What are their names? Where do they go to school?
- What color car do you drive? Where is it parked?
- How much money do you have in your bank account?

How does this line of questioning feel? What will you say? Will you give those answers? Will you lie?

How long will you stand there before screaming at the person to get away from you or before running away? This is exactly how stakeholders feel when you begin your discovery conversations by asking hard questions that go too far below the surface.

It is human nature to put up an emotional wall when strangers start asking difficult, intrusive questions. In your role as a salesperson, you are the stranger. When you ask questions that make your stakeholders uncomfortable before you have established trust, their emotional wall goes up, and they shut down.

The key to breaking through emotional walls is beginning discovery conversations with questions that are easy for your stakeholders to answer and that they will enjoy answering. This is why it is crucial that you do your research on stakeholders in advance and prepare easy questions that they will enjoy answering.

The more you become genuinely interested in stakeholders, the more valuable and important they feel. The better they feel, the more they will want to talk. The more they talk and you listen, the more connected they will feel to you. As you connect, you gain the right to ask the deeper questions that get below the surface.

The Pump and Pounce

The most destructive sales behavior during discovery conversations is the annoying tendency of pumping stakeholders for information with interrogating, closed-ended questions, and then pouncing on the first chance to start pitching. Born from impatience and poor impulse control, this one habit will cause you to miss important clues, damage relationships, and lose out on sales.

Here's how it works. During discovery, in response to a question, your stakeholder says, "We've been having a hard time with [fill in the blank]." Rather than asking deeper probing questions to gain clarity and understanding, you pounce and start pitching solutions. As soon as you start pitching, your ears turn off, and so does your stakeholder.

The key to effective discovery conversations is patiently asking questions, encouraging stakeholders to talk, and getting all the information on the table before formulating any recommendations or offering solutions. In longer-cycle sales, discovery may span many meetings with multiple stakeholders before any presentation or recommended solutions are offered. This is a key reason you need to take good notes.

Failure to Prepare

Discovery is a language of questions. But effective discovery doesn't just happen. To be effective, to be valuable, you must do your research and plan your approach in advance, before you ever ask the first question. Trust us on this; when it comes to discovery, winging it is stupid.

The most egregious mistake with discovery is the failure to prepare for discovery meetings. Your lack of preparation will shine through in your weak, disjointed questions. Stakeholders will know that you didn't care enough to do your research and develop your questions. You will come off as a hack rather than a professional consultant. You'll waste time rather than creating value.

This is a huge irritation to buyers. According to studies by Blender and SiriusDecisions, about 80% of B2B buyers complain that salespeople are unprepared for meetings. This includes complaints that salespeople know nothing about their prospects' companies or industries. Salespeople reveal their failure to prepare by asking questions that research could have answered.

The real secret to effective discovery conversations is planning. Pre-call planning can be an extensive strategic process for large, complex deals, or it can be simple and straightforward for short-cycle, low-complexity opportunities. Regardless of your deal size and cycle, discovery call planning will focus on three key areas:

1. What you already know
2. What you want to learn
3. Understanding stakeholders and their motivations

The primary reason why salespeople fail to prepare for discovery meetings is that it requires effort and discipline. It is important to note that AI will not have this discipline for you. Only you can choose to have the discipline to do pre-call planning for your discovery meetings.

What AI can do is make the process much easier by doing the heavy lifting on research and speeding up the process. It can help you gain insights into your stakeholders' industries, companies, and challenges. It can even help you develop some of your discovery questions in advance. Over the course of the next two chapters, we'll tackle how to use artificial intelligence for pre-call research and developing discovery questions.

33

Pre-Discovery-Call Research

Tony's company helps clients hire top-tier talent with hiring assessments. When Tony and his team were courting a large furniture seller, they shopped the company first. "We went into the store and took in the entire experience. By posing as customers we learned about their sales process, the types of people they hire, and their culture."

Tony continued, "When we showed up for our initial discovery meeting, we explained to the stakeholder group what we had done. They were beyond impressed that we'd invested time to get to know them. You could feel the emotional shift in the room. We walked in as salespeople and out as consultants. Today, they are one of our largest customers."

Before discovery conversations, learn everything possible about the organization and the people you are meeting with in advance. Leverage AI, social media, your CRM, and the internet to gather information about stakeholders and their organizations. This has five benefits:

1. It helps you avoid asking stupid questions that demonstrate your lack of preparation.
2. It helps you craft easy questions that get your stakeholder talking.
3. You learn to speak your prospect's language.
4. It makes your stakeholder feel important because you provide tangible evidence that you cared enough to invest effort in getting to know them.
5. Through preplanning you begin to develop theories and hypotheses that can be tested through questioning.

When you have an understanding of your prospective client's industry, business, or challenges, you position yourself as the expert consultant and authority who can solve their problems.

Needs Something or Knows Something

Many salespeople are under the false impression that discovery is about acquiring information from their prospect that will help them get from "hello" to "closed" as rapidly as possible. These self-oriented, "needs something" sellers demonstrate through their shallowness and lack of research that they care only about themselves and achieving their own outcomes. They care less about what the prospective client says and more about how they can use what they say to pitch a solution.

By contrast, "knows something" sellers like Tony, from the story that opens this chapter, bring knowledge, research, expertise, and insight into discovery conversations. They ask thoughtful, artful, and strategic questions that are developed from their research. Like consultants, their questions serve a dual purpose, sparking their prospect's awareness of the need to change, and gathering important information so they can develop solutions and a business case.

Proving yourself to be a "knows-something" salesperson requires doing your homework about your prospect, their industry, and the headwinds and tailwinds they face. Great discovery conversations begin with you taking an assessment of the things you already know and researching the things that you can know without asking a single question.

Start with What You Already Know

Before any discovery conversation, you should review the notes in your CRM. Perhaps there are entries there from past salespeople who have worked the account. There should also be notes you have made from prospecting interactions and previous conversations.

This of course raises the fact that if you are not taking notes during conversations with stakeholders, you are committing sales malpractice (and we are likely to report you to the authorities). There is no possible way that you will ever remember every conversation, and we know what happens when you ask questions you have already asked.

These days AI note takers abound. There are dozens of good options, including Otter.ai, Chorus.ai, and the AI note takers that are built into platforms like Zoom, Teams, and Google Meets. These apps continue to get better and better at providing both full transcriptions and summaries.

When meeting with stakeholders in person, apps like Otter.ai can take notes for you. Just pull up the app on your phone and ask permission to record. Then, following your meeting, upload the meeting notes into your CRM.

I use AI note takers in every meeting. I find the summaries to be hugely valuable for preparing for my next meeting and building proposals. But I also take notes by hand using a digital tablet called reMarkable. Following meetings, I convert my handwritten notes to digital text and upload them into my CRM. I also run them through ChatGPT to generate a bullet-pointed summary.

There are a number of reasons I take notes by hand, even though I have an AI that also is taking notes:

- **Understanding:** Writing by hand is proven to help you process information, which can lead to a deeper comprehension of the conversation.[1]

- **Improved memory:** The act of writing activates areas of the brain that help increase comprehension and retention.[2]

- **Boosts creativity:** Writing by hand activates the creative center of your brain, which helps you develop better solutions for your prospect. It helps you leverage your human advantage to think out of the box and differentiate from your competitors.

- **Reduces distractions:** When you are taking notes by hand you are less likely to become distracted, so you can stay focused on your stakeholders.

- **Relationships:** When you take notes by hand it makes people feel important and that you care, deepening human connections.

- **Respect:** Recently the CFO of my company decided that we would not do business with a vendor after their sales rep typed their way through a discovery meeting

---

[1] Charlotte Hu, "Why Writing by Hand Is Better for Memory and Learning," *Scientific American,* February 21, 2024, https://www.scientificamerican.com/article/why-writing-by-hand-is-better-for-memory-and-learning
[2] Ibid.

on their laptop. She said, "I don't even think they were listening to me!" Typing notes into your laptop or tablet is rude and disrespectful.

Taking good notes and being disciplined enough to consistently record new information into your CRM makes pre-discovery-call planning much easier. The CRM exists so you don't have to remember things, but it cannot remember what you don't put into it. It is a record of your interactions and your relationships.

In the near future, the AI built into your CRM will be able to do much of this legwork for you by summarizing the things you already know. It will even make recommendations for information that you might need to learn, along with questions you should ask. But the information it gives you is only as good as the information you have provided it. Remember Robot Rule Two: Crap in, crap out.

Research for Information You Can Know Without Asking

Research and qualifying go hand in hand. With AI assisting you, there is absolutely no excuse for not doing extensive research on every prospect and stakeholder before you ever engage in a discovery conversation or put them into your pipeline. The things you'll want to research include:

- **Company:** What it does, whom it serves, business strengths and weaknesses, business strategies, SEC filings, stock performance, business initiatives, challenges, vendors, software providers, footprint, how they differentiate, and so on
- **Stakeholders:** Who they are, their roles, tenure, career and educational backgrounds, hobbies, motivations; key players in the company that you may want to meet or know
- **Industry:** Trends, challenges, headwinds, tailwinds, jargon, risks, opportunities

- **Competitors:** Who are the top competitors, how do the competitors compare, how do they differentiate, strengths and weaknesses

AI is brilliant at research. All you need to do is give it the right prompt and you'll get the information you are seeking in seconds. The optimal word here is *right*. As we've repeated often, the quality of information AI gives you is directly correlated to the quality of the prompt you give it.

A word of warning when it comes to the information you get from your AI. Never forget Robot Rule One: *Never trust, always verify*. AI hallucinates. It will give you false information. It will sometimes outright lie. Therefore you'll want to do multiple searches for the information on different platforms, including directly in search engines.

Examples of Research Prompts

You
Give me a summary of salesgravy.com website

ChatGPT
SalesGravy.com is a website dedicated to enhancing the performance of sales teams and individuals through a variety of training and development services. Founded in 2006 by Jeb Blount, a renowned author and sales expert, the platform is recognized globally for its comprehensive sales training and enablement solutions.

The services offered by Sales Gravy include a wide range of instructor-led training courses, workshops, and e-learning options through Sales Gravy University. These cover various sales-related topics such as prospecting, negotiating, selling in volatile times, and mastering sales objections. Additionally, they provide virtual selling skills training which is crucial in today's digital-first business environment.

Sales Gravy also emphasizes the development of sales leadership and coaching skills, offering specific training for sales managers and executives to build high-performing teams. Beyond training, the platform provides resources like sales playbooks, compensation strategies, and hiring assessments, aiming to accelerate sales productivity and organizational agility.

For those interested in continuous learning, Sales Gravy offers an extensive catalog of on-demand courses available online, allowing sales professionals to learn at their own pace and on any device. The platform caters to a broad audience, from frontline salespeople to top-level executives, ensuring that every level of a sales organization can benefit from their offerings (SalesGravy) (SalesGravy).

Provide me with a list of the hiring and staffing challenges faced by small and medium engineering firms

Small and medium engineering firms often face several hiring and staffing challenges, including:

1. Limited resources: These firms typically have smaller budgets and fewer resources compared to larger organizations, making it challenging to offer competitive compensation packages and attract top talent.

2. Difficulty in attracting specialized talent: Engineering projects often require specific expertise and skills, which can be difficult to find in the local talent pool, especially for niche or emerging technologies.

3. Competition with larger firms: Larger engineering firms may offer better benefits, higher salaries, and more opportunities for career growth, making it harder for smaller firms to compete for the same pool of candidates.

4. Limited brand recognition: Smaller firms may have lower brand recognition, which can make it harder to attract candidates who are seeking well-known and reputable employers.

5. Lack of dedicated human resources department: Many small and medium engineering firms do not have a dedicated human resources department, which can make it challenging to manage the recruitment process efficiently and effectively.

6. Limited training and development opportunities: Smaller firms may have fewer resources to invest in training and professional development programs, which can make it harder to attract and retain top talent.

7. Project-based hiring: Engineering firms often hire employees based on specific project needs, which can lead to a high turnover rate and the need for frequent recruitment efforts.

8. Geographic limitations: Smaller firms may be limited to a specific geographic area, reducing the available talent pool and making it harder to find qualified candidates.

9. Work-life balance challenges: Engineering projects can be demanding, with long hours and tight deadlines, which can make it challenging to maintain a healthy work-life balance, potentially deterring candidates who prioritize this aspect.

10. Managing remote or hybrid work arrangements: With the increasing prevalence of remote and hybrid work models, smaller firms may face challenges in effectively managing and integrating remote employees or coordinating hybrid teams.

To overcome these challenges, small and medium engineering firms may need to be creative in their recruitment strategies, leverage their unique strengths (such as a more personalized work environment or specialized expertise), and invest in effective talent management practices.

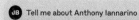

Anthony Iannarino is a well-known figure in the sales and business world. Here are some key points about him:

1. Sales Expert: He is a highly regarded sales leader, speaker, and author who specializes in B2B sales strategies.

2. Author: Iannarino has written several bestselling books on sales, including "The Only Sales Guide You'll Ever Need," "The Lost Art of Closing," and "Eat Their Lunch: Winning Customers Away from Your Competition."

3. Speaker: He is a sought-after keynote speaker at sales conferences and corporate events worldwide.

4. Blogger: Iannarino maintains a popular sales blog where he regularly shares insights and advice on sales strategies, leadership, and personal development.

5. Consultant: He works as a sales consultant, helping organizations improve their sales processes and strategies.

6. Sales Leadership: He has a background in sales leadership, having served as the President of SOLUTIONS Staffing for many years.

7. Podcast Host: Iannarino hosts "In the Arena," a podcast focused on sales and personal development topics.

8. Education: He holds a Master's degree in English Literature, which he often credits for his ability to communicate effectively in sales.

9. Philosophy: His sales philosophy emphasizes the importance of creating value for clients, building strong relationships, and continuous personal development.

10. Influence: Iannarino is widely recognized as one of the top influencers in the sales industry, known for his practical, no-nonsense approach to sales techniques and strategies.

Anthony Iannarino's work has significantly impacted the modern understanding of B2B sales strategies and techniques, making him a respected voice in the sales community.

Copy Retry

Claude can make mistakes. Please double-check responses.

You

What is ZoomInfo's core value proposition?

ChatGPT

ZoomInfo's core value proposition revolves around providing comprehensive and high-quality business data and insights to empower organizations to accelerate their sales and marketing efforts. Here are some key aspects of what ZoomInfo offers:

1. **B2B Contact and Company Data**: ZoomInfo maintains an extensive database of business contacts and company information. This data includes direct dial phone numbers, email addresses, and other relevant details that enable sales and marketing professionals to reach out to potential clients and decision-makers effectively.
2. **Sales Intelligence and Prospecting Tools**: ZoomInfo provides tools that help sales teams identify and target potential customers who are more likely to be interested in their products or services. This includes features like lead scoring, intent signals, and trigger events that indicate a prospect's readiness to buy.
3. **Marketing Automation Integration**: The platform integrates with various marketing automation and customer relationship management (CRM) systems. This seamless integration allows for the synchronization of data across platforms, enabling more efficient and coordinated sales and marketing campaigns.
4. **Advanced Analytics and Reporting**: ZoomInfo offers analytics tools that help businesses track the effectiveness of their sales and marketing efforts. These tools provide insights into campaign performance, lead generation, and conversion rates, assisting companies in making data-driven decisions.
5. **Compliance and Data Privacy**: In an era where data privacy is critical, ZoomInfo places a strong emphasis on compliance with regulations such as GDPR and CCPA. This commitment helps ensure that users can trust the data they receive and use it responsibly.

Overall, ZoomInfo's value proposition is about leveraging detailed, actionable data to improve business outreach, accelerate sales cycles, and enhance marketing efforts, all while maintaining a focus on data quality and compliance.

You

What are CEOs in the temporary staffing industry most worried about this year?

ChatGPT

In 2024, CEOs in the temporary staffing industry are particularly concerned with several key issues:

1. **Economic Uncertainty**: With the effects of past economic downturns lingering, CEOs are wary of potential recession impacts and hesitant market conditions, which can influence the stability of staffing demands across various sectors.
2. **Regulatory Changes and Compliance**: New regulations and compliance requirements, particularly those related to employment laws and worker classification, are a significant concern. These can affect operational processes and necessitate adjustments in business models to ensure compliance.
3. **Technology Adoption and Cybersecurity**: The integration of advanced technologies, especially AI-driven platforms for talent engagement and management, is becoming crucial. However, this also raises concerns about cybersecurity and the protection of sensitive data.
4. **Talent Shortage and Workforce Management**: A consistent issue is the shortage of qualified candidates for certain roles. Additionally, managing a workforce that increasingly values flexibility, including remote and hybrid work arrangements, is a strategic focus area to address.
5. **Impact of Political Events**: With 2024 being an election year in the U.S., political uncertainties can affect business and hiring practices, as companies may adopt a wait-and-see approach to understand the potential impacts of new policies.

These insights suggest that while there are challenges, there are also ample opportunities for innovation and strategic adjustments within the industry to navigate these concerns effectively (Staffing Industry Review).

EXERCISE 33.1: RESEARCH A PROSPECT

Think about a prospect in your pipeline with which you have a scheduled discovery call. Take a moment now to conduct pre-discovery-call research using the following questions. For each one, write an AI prompt you can use to get started.

1. **Research the company:** What they do, how they differentiate, current initiatives, value proposition, history, go-to-market strategies, and risks they must publish if it is a public company.
   Prompt: _____
   _____
   _____

2. **Research their industry:** Identify trends and challenges. What are executives in this industry worried about?
   Prompt: _____
   _____
   _____

3. **Competitors:** Who are their top competitors and how they differentiate, current initiatives, value proposition, history, and go-to-market strategies.
   Prompt: _____
   _____
   _____

4. **Stakeholders:** Do background research on all the company stakeholders who will be in the discovery meeting. Get to know other executives who may have authority over the stakeholders in your meeting.
   Prompt: _____
   _____
   _____

34

Discovery Questions: What You Want to Learn

If discovery had its own language, it would be a language of questions. In sales, a question you ask is more important than anything you will ever say, and anything you can say is more impactful when delivered in the form of a question.

The quality and depth of your discovery questions have the greatest impact on whether you win or lose a deal. Effective discovery is asking the right questions, at the right time, to the right people. And the right questions, are open-ended questions.

The Power of Open-Ended Questions

Open-ended questions like "How is that impacting you?" or "What happens when your workers' compensation costs increase?" encourage prospects to talk and elaborate—to tell stories.

Conversely, closed-ended questions like "How many of those do you use?" or "Are you happy with that?" elicit short, limited responses. Closed-ended questions are self-serving and interrogative, because they are primarily focused on you—getting only the information you need to rev up your pitch.

Most salespeople have at least a rudimentary understanding of open- and closed-ended question types. If you were to interview 100 sales professionals, 99 of them would tell you that open-ended questions are most effective in sales conversations. Yet if you were to observe these same salespeople interacting with stakeholders, you'd mostly hear interrogating, closed-ended questions.

Closed-ended questions become habitual because they're easy, give you the illusion of control, and require little intellectual effort and even less emotional investment. Salespeople who find it hard to ask open-ended questions tend to share certain characteristics:

- They are unable to manage their disruptive emotional attachment to always being in control.
- They are unwilling to let go and just allow the conversation to happen with the faith that their prospect will reveal key information inside the context of the stories stakeholders tell you about their unique situation.
- They lack the discipline to focus their attention on the other person.
- They find it easier to ask closed-ended questions that elicit bullet points rather than allow stakeholders to express themselves and then truly listen.

In sales, 99 percent of your questions should be open-ended. This includes questioning statements like "Tell me more" or "Walk me through that process." The statement-and-pause approach is particularly effective for getting prospects to talk. It works like this: Say something like "Wow, it sounds like that's been really challenging." Then pause and allow silence to do the rest of the work.

This technique will serve you in two ways. First, it demonstrates that you are listening. Second, the other person almost always fills in the silence with a story.

The objective of the open-ended question is to elicit stories. Within these stories you gain access to the information you need to build your case, and insight into what is most important to your stakeholder. It is through these stories that stakeholders teach you their language and the root causes of the problems you can help them solve.

AI Can Assist with Discovery Questions

The primary objective of discovery is to gather the information you need to put your business case puzzle together. Some of the information you need to build your case will be revealed as you do research, while the bulk of it will come to the surface during discovery conversations with your stakeholders.

Therefore, before engaging in discovery conversations, you must have a clear understanding of what you want to learn. With your "what you want to learn" objective defined, you can develop and practice the questions you will ask in advance.

AI can assist you with developing discovery questions as long as you provide it the right information and prompts. *Assist* is the optimal word here. Because discovery is so fundamental to developing relationships with stakeholders, turning it over entirely to your AI is a colossal mistake. For this reason, it is crucial that you review and refine the questions that AI gives you so that your discovery meetings are conversations rather than interrogations. You want your questions to flow together and build on one another.

Our favorite AI prompts for building discovery questions are structured to include the following information:

- What you sell
- The market you sell into
- The stakeholder roles in your meeting
- The type and size of the company
- That you want open-ended questions
- What you want those questions to uncover

Here is an example:

 You

I sell PEO solutions to small and medium sized businesses. I'm conducting a discovery meeting with the CEO and CFO of a $10,000,000 HVAC company. Give me ten open-ended questions that I can ask that will help me uncover their hiring, employee retention, and payroll challenges while demonstrating that I understand the HVAC industry.

ChatGPT

Absolutely! Crafting the right questions for your discovery meeting is crucial for understanding how your PEO solutions can best serve the HVAC company. Here are ten open-ended questions designed to uncover their needs in hiring, employee retention, and payroll management, while also showing your understanding of the HVAC industry:

1. **Workforce Dynamics and Seasonality**
   "How does your workforce need to adjust during peak seasons, and what challenges do you face in scaling up or down?"

2. **Recruitment Strategies**
   "What methods have you found most effective for recruiting skilled HVAC technicians, and what gaps are you currently experiencing in your recruitment process?"

3. **Employee Retention**
   "What are the primary reasons employees leave your company, and what retention strategies have you found most effective or ineffective?"

4. **Payroll Management Complexity**
   "How do you currently manage payroll and compliance across different states or regions, and what are the biggest pain points in this process?"

5. **Benefits and Employee Satisfaction**
   "What type of benefits package do you offer, and how well do you think it aligns with the expectations of your current and potential employees?"

6. **Compliance and Regulatory Challenges**
   "What specific regulatory compliance issues have you found most burdensome, and how are you currently handling these challenges?"

7. **Technology and Process Efficiency**
   "How satisfied are you with the technology and systems currently in place for HR and payroll management? Where do you see potential for improvement?"

8. **Impact of Company Culture**
   "Can you describe your company culture and how it impacts employee productivity and job satisfaction?"

9. **Financial Planning and Employee Costs**
   "How do you approach budgeting for employee costs, such as wages, benefits, and training, especially during fluctuations in business volume?"

.0. **Future Workforce Planning**
   "Looking ahead, what are the key workforce challenges you anticipate as your business grows, and how are you planning to address them?"

Real Situation Questions

During discovery conversations, stakeholders will obfuscate and hide the truth about what is really happening. They do this for various reasons, including embarrassment, delusion, and the belief that if they reveal what is really going on, you will use it against them.

Sometimes your stakeholder—especially if they are a top-level executive—is so removed and disconnected from the day-to-day business that they don't actually see the problems. This is exactly why you must spend time with multiple stakeholders, go through a discovery process before demos, tour facilities, spend a day observing how they do business, and dive into the data to get the true story.

In every deal, the one alternative that is always on the table is staying put—doing nothing. In fact, the majority of lost deals are lost to "no decision" because the stakeholder felt no compelling reason to change. For this reason, you must dig deep to understand the *real* current state of affairs.

Because the status quo is almost always perceived by stakeholders as the strongest alternative to change, you must make it your mission to eliminate "no decision" as an alternative by asking questions that bring the real situation to the surface and help stakeholders become aware of why the status quo is untenable. Here is an example of how AI can help you with *real-situation* questions:

Root-Cause Analysis Questions

Getting to the root cause of your prospect's problems is the key to developing a set of personalized solutions to present to the stakeholder group. What's important to understand is that many times stakeholders don't know the root cause of their problems because they are too close to those problems.

Strategic root-cause questions put you in the position of an expert consultant. These types of questions get below the surface and explore data, systems, processes, and methodologies. They help you uncover the changes that will be required to help your prospect achieve their desired outcomes. Here is an example of how AI can help you develop root-cause analysis questions.

Measurable Business Outcomes

Identifying measurable business outcomes (MBO) and gaining consensus on the value of those outcomes—the metrics that matter—are the keys to developing a winning business case and proposal.[1]

---

[1]Jeb Blount, *INKED: The Ultimate Guide to Powerful Closing and Sales Negotiation Tactics that Unlock YES and Seal the Deal* (Hoboken, NJ: Wiley), 2020.

Some of these MBOs will be out in the open and readily identified by the stakeholder group. Others will need to be surfaced with artful strategic questions that help stakeholders become aware of the opportunity to create MBOs that can transform their business.

When you have intimate knowledge of the metrics that matter to your stakeholder group, it's much easier to use your calculator to demonstrate the value of your proposal in black and white. The more tangible the MBOs, the stronger the case is for doing business with you and the higher the probability that you will close the sale. Here's an example of how AI can help you develop MBO questions:

ChatGPT

For a discovery meeting with the head of sales at a heavy equipment dealer, your questions should focus on understanding their current processes, identifying pain points, and exploring the potential benefits of CRM integration. Here are five targeted questions designed to elicit information that can guide a productive conversation about implementing your CRM software:

1. **Current Sales Process Insights**
   "Can you walk me through your current sales process from lead generation to closing? What are the biggest challenges your sales team faces in managing and nurturing these leads?"

2. **Data Utilization and Reporting**
   "How do you currently track and manage customer interactions, and what tools do you use for sales forecasting and reporting? Are there specific data insights you feel you're missing that could drive better decision-making?"

3. **Customer Retention and Satisfaction**
   "What strategies do you currently employ to ensure customer retention and satisfaction? How do you measure the success of these strategies, and where do you see room for improvement?"

4. **Integration and Workflow Optimization**
   "How well are your current tools integrated into your sales and customer service workflows? Are there any repetitive tasks or information bottlenecks that you think could be streamlined with better technology?"

5. **Business Outcomes and ROI**
   "What specific business outcomes are you aiming to achieve in the next year, and how do you see a new CRM system supporting these goals? Additionally, what metrics or KPIs are most important to you when assessing the ROI of new sales technologies?"

Paradigm-Shift and Future State Aspirations Questions

Future state questions are designed to help stakeholders see a better future and drive their motivation to change. These questions compel stakeholders to articulate their vision for the future.

Paradigm shift questions help stakeholders get prepared to move beyond the status quo. These questions encourage them to step into the changes they need to make at a strategic level to move into this better future. Here is an example of how AI can help you develop these types of questions:

---

⑨ **ChatGPT**

When working with a law firm concerned about the costs of moving to a larger, more prestigious building, it's essential to use questions that help them visualize the benefits and long-term gains of such a transition. Here are five open-ended questions designed to help them think through and embrace the potential advantages of moving to a new space:

1. **Vision and Growth Alignment**
   "Can you describe what an ideal office space would look like for your firm, considering your plans for growth and the image you want to project to clients?"
2. **Current Limitations**
   "How does your current space limit your firm's operations or the services you can provide to your clients? What opportunities do you think you might be missing due to these limitations?"
3. **Client Perception and Firm Prestige**
   "How important is the location and appearance of your office to your clients? In what ways could a more modern and strategically located office enhance your firm's reputation and attract new business?"
4. **Future Space Utilization**
   "Looking ahead, what additional capabilities or services would you like to incorporate into your practice that your current building cannot accommodate? How could a new space better serve those needs?"
5. **Cost Consideration and Investment Perspective**
   "While considering the initial costs of moving, have you thought about the potential return on investment from increased client intake and higher employee satisfaction and productivity in a new, modern space?"

↓

Vendor and Value-Evaluation Questions

It's important that you understand what your prospect values and how they will select the vendor of choice. These questions elicit beliefs, expectations, and preferences for the vendors your stakeholders prefer to partner with. With this information, you'll gain insight on how to build your business case and proposal, to align with their values and evaluation criteria. Here is an example of how AI can help you with these types of questions:

 You

I sell janitorial and facility services. I have a discovery meeting with the Director of Operations for a 100 person accounting and consulting firm. She is looking for a new janitorial vendor for their office building and conducting meetings with several of my competitors. Please give me some questions that will help me gain a better understand of the criteria she will use to choose a vendor of choice along with her company's core values.

ChatGPT

In a competitive scenario like the one you're describing, it's crucial to ask questions that not only uncover the Director of Operations' specific criteria for choosing a janitorial vendor but also align your services with the core values of their company. Here are some questions that can help you position your services effectively:

1. **Understanding Service Expectations**

   "Can you describe what you are looking for in a janitorial service? What specific aspects of the service provided by your previous vendor would you like to see improved?"

2. **Criteria for Vendor Selection**

   "What are the most important factors you will consider when selecting a new janitorial vendor? Are there any particular qualifications or certifications that you require?"

3. **Alignment with Company Values**

   "How do the core values of your firm influence your expectations for vendors and partners? Could you share examples of how these values might translate into the janitorial services you are seeking?"

4. **Communication and Reporting Preferences**

   "What type of communication and reporting do you expect from your janitorial service provider? How frequently do you expect updates, and through which channels?"

5. **Feedback and Quality Assurance Processes**

   "How do you prefer to handle feedback and quality assurance with your vendors? What does the ideal process look like for addressing any concerns that may arise?"

EXERCISE 34.1: DEVELOP DISCOVERY QUESTIONS

Now it's time for you to prompt your AI to help you develop questions for an upcoming discovery meeting.

1. Think about a prospect in your pipeline with which you have a scheduled discovery call.
2. Determine the "What you need to learn" objective of your meeting.
3. Use a variety of prompts with your AI to help you develop 10 questions that align with your objective.
4. In the left column of this table, make a list of the questions AI developed for you in the order that you plan to ask them.
5. In the right column, edit and hone the AI-generated questions to sound more conversational and human.

What You Need to Learn Objective:	
AI-Generated Question	**Human-Edited/Honed Question**

Stakeholder Success Criteria Questions

Each stakeholder will have their own personal success criteria, problems they want to solve, and ideas and feelings on the status quo and alternatives to doing business with you. Some of these criteria will be logical and some emotional. But because emotions drive buying decisions, it is crucial that you uncover and address individual stakeholder criteria, with questions like these:

- "Tell me what success means to you?"
- "Can you tell me about what's most important to you?"
- "What problems are you personally trying to solve?"
- "What worries you most about the current situation?"
- "Can you walk me through the alternatives you feel are available to solve these problems?"
- "What would change for you personally if this initiative is successful?"

Stakeholders play different roles in the buying process and their companies. Their specific role and responsibilities affect their personal motivations and biases. Therefore it is essential that you are familiar with the common motivational patterns and decision-making thought processes of C-level executives to middle managers.

Sometimes, though, you'll encounter a stakeholder who has a title, role, or responsibility that you are unfamiliar with. AI can give you insight into what is important to them prior to going into a discovery meeting. Here is an example of a stakeholder insight prompt:

You

I sell environmental services. I'm meeting with the plant manager for a hospital laundry facility for the first time. Please give me insight into what will be important to this person and their personal motivations.

ChatGPT

When meeting with a plant manager of a hospital laundry facility, it's important to understand their unique position and the pressures they face. The priorities of a plant manager in this context likely revolve around operational efficiency, compliance with health and environmental regulations, cost management, and ensuring the safety and effectiveness of the laundry processes. Here are key areas that might be important to them and could drive their personal motivations:

1. **Regulatory Compliance**: Compliance with both environmental and health safety standards is crucial in a hospital setting. The plant manager would be motivated to maintain high standards to avoid legal issues and potential fines.
2. **Operational Efficiency**: They will be focused on optimizing laundry operations to handle large volumes efficiently while minimizing downtime, which affects the hospital's overall functionality.
3. **Cost Effectiveness**: Cost control is a significant concern, particularly in how energy, water, and chemicals are used in the laundry process. They will be interested in any service that can reduce these costs.
4. **Sustainability**: Environmental impact is a growing concern in all sectors, including healthcare. The manager will likely be motivated by opportunities to enhance sustainability practices, reducing waste and using eco-friendly chemicals and processes.
5. **Quality Assurance**: Ensuring that the laundering process meets the high standards required for hospital linens in terms of hygiene and cleanliness is crucial. They must prevent any cross-contamination or infection risks.
6. **Staff Safety and Morale**: The plant manager will also be concerned about the safety and efficiency of their staff. Solutions that make the workplace safer and improve morale could be very appealing.
7. **Technological Advancements**: They might be motivated to keep up with the latest technology in terms of machinery and automation that can improve efficiency and quality.

When discussing your environmental services, highlight how they align with these areas of concern—especially how they can help the facility maintain compliance, enhance operational efficiency, and promote sustainability. This approach not only addresses the plant manager's professional responsibilities but also aligns with personal motivations to excel in their role and contribute positively to the broader goals of the hospital.

EXERCISE 34.2: STAKEHOLDER MOTIVATIONS

In this exercise you will explore individual stakeholder success criteria and what motivates them.

1. Think about a prospect in your pipeline with which you have a scheduled discovery call during which more than two stakeholders will be present.
2. List each stakeholder and their job title in the table below.
3. Write down what you perceive as each stakeholder's success criteria.
4. Prompt your AI about each stakeholder's success criteria and motivations and compare notes.
5. Develop discovery questions for each stakeholder based on your research and intuition.

Stakeholder	Title	What You Think Motivates Them (Success Criteria)	What AI Thinks Motivates Them (Success Criteria)	Discovery Questions to Uncover Success Criteria

By the time you've completed your pre-discovery-call research, you should have a good foundation for your conversation. Not only will you understand the prospective company and their industry, but you may also have some clues about the concerns and priorities of the stakeholders you meet with.

PART 7

Close the Deal

I often tell my students not to be misled by the name "artificial intelligence"— there is nothing artificial about it. AI is made by humans, intended to behave by humans, and, ultimately, to impact humans' lives and human society.

—*Fei-Fei Li*

35

Competitive Analysis and Objection Prevention

This book is focused squarely on helping you leverage artificial intelligence to sell more. Like any technology or competitive weapon, though, the race is on and everyone will be using it to save time and make better decisions.

Your prospects, for example, as they consider their alternatives when making buying decisions, may use AI to compare you to your competitors. What they find can result in tough, challenging questions that may set you back on your heels during final presentations, along with buying commitment objections that surface when you attempt to close the sale.

This is an example of a prompt stakeholders might use for their research: "Compare the positives and negatives of these two banks: JP Morgan Chase and CitiGroup for an SMB [small or mid-sized business] company in Oklahoma." Here is what the prompt returned:

JP Morgan Chase

Positives:

1. Wide Range of Services: JP Morgan Chase offers a comprehensive suite of financial services, including banking, lending, investment, and wealth management solutions, which can cater to various needs of SMBs.
2. Strong Reputation: JP Morgan Chase has a long-standing reputation as one of the largest and most reputable banks globally, which can provide credibility and trust to SMBs.
3. National Presence: With branches and ATMs spread across the country, including Oklahoma, SMBs can access banking services conveniently.
4. Technology and Innovation: JP Morgan Chase invests heavily in technology and offers advanced digital banking solutions, which can streamline financial management for SMBs.
5. Specialized SMB Services: The bank provides specialized services tailored for small and mid-sized businesses, such as business credit cards, merchant services, and payroll solutions.

Negatives:

1. Higher Fees: Some of JP Morgan Chase's services may come with higher fees compared to smaller banks or credit unions, which can impact the cost-effectiveness for SMBs.
2. Limited Personalization: Despite offering a wide range of services, JP Morgan Chase's approach might not be as personalized as a smaller, community-focused bank, potentially leading to a less tailored experience for SMBs.

CitiGroup

Positives:

1. Global Presence: CitiGroup operates in numerous countries, providing SMBs with access to international banking services, trade finance, and global market insights.

2. Innovative Solutions: CitiGroup is known for its innovative financial products and services, including digital banking platforms and specialized business solutions.

3. Flexible Financing: The bank offers various lending options tailored to SMBs, including lines of credit, term loans, and commercial mortgages, which can help facilitate business growth.

4. Diverse Product Portfolio: CitiGroup offers a diverse range of financial products beyond traditional banking, such as investment banking, treasury and trade solutions, and risk management services.

5. Strong Brand Recognition: Similar to JP Morgan Chase, CitiGroup enjoys strong brand recognition globally, which can provide reassurance and trust to SMBs.

Negatives:

1. Limited Branch Network: While CitiGroup has a significant presence in major cities, its branch network might be less extensive compared to regional banks, which can affect accessibility for SMBs, especially in rural areas of Oklahoma.

2. Complexity: CitiGroup's extensive range of products and services may introduce complexity, and SMBs might find it challenging to navigate through the offerings to find the most suitable solutions.

3. Risk of Concentration: Relying heavily on a global banking giant like CitiGroup might expose SMBs to systemic risks

associated with the bank's global operations, regulatory environment, and market fluctuations.

AI can also put this same information in an easy-to-digest table:

You

Can you put this in a table format for me?

ChatGPT

Sure, here's the comparison in a table format:

Aspect	JP Morgan Chase	Citi Group
Positives		
Wide Range of Services	✓	✓
Strong Reputation	✓	✓
National Presence	✓	
Technology and Innovation	✓	✓
Specialized SMB Services	✓	
Negatives		
Higher Fees	✓	
Limited Personalization	✓	
Global Presence		✓
Innovative Solutions		✓
Flexible Financing		✓
Diverse Product Portfolio		✓
Limited Branch Network		✓
Complexity		✓
Risk of Concentration		✓

Buyers researching with AI is the new norm. If you walk into a presentation or closing meeting only to be blindsided by tough questions about your competitive weaknesses, that is on you. Therefore, it is in your best interest to do the same research and prepare in advance to answer difficult questions and neutralize objections. Get started with Exercise 35.1.

EXERCISE 35.1: LEVERAGE AI TO ANALYZE YOUR COMPETITORS

If prospects are doing this type of research, you can bet your commission check that savvy competitors are going to use AI to find and exploit your company's weaknesses. Don't wait until you are pushed in a corner. Get to work now and analyze each of your competitors in relation to each other and your company. Here are some potential prompts to get you started:

- Summarize [competitor] website.
- Concisely describe [competitor] and its primary solution. Enumerate the main features and capabilities.
- What problems does [competitor] solve?
- What is [competitor's] unique value proposition? How is it unique compared to other market offerings?
- Describe the strengths and weaknesses of [competitor]. Highlight significant shortcomings.
- Summarize common negative user or customer feedback for [competitor].
- Explore current market conditions affecting [competitor].
- Compare the strengths and weaknesses of these two companies: [competitor] and [your company]
- I'm a sales professional. My competitor is [company name]. Tell me [competitor's] weaknesses and how to exploit them.

Review the information you learned in Exercise 35.1 and develop questions and messaging to use during discovery conversations and presentations to subtly and systematically eliminate your competitors as an alternative in the minds of your prospect's stakeholders.

36

AI-Powered Proposals

It is the moment of truth. You've completed discovery and are at the point in the sales process where you present your proposal to stakeholders. You know that two of your competitors are still being considered.

Once you walk your contacts through a presentation and hand off your proposal, you may not have another chance to ensure you win the business. This is a high-stakes game with only one winner, and you want that winner to be you. There are a number of strategies that can increase your chances of closing the sale:

- **Preparing for Your Presentation and Proposal:** Before your final presentation, review what you have learned with your key contact and ask them what they feel is most important. Prepare your presentation to address these topics and concerns.

- **Check Your Work:** It is embarrassing to open PowerPoint only to find that the company name was the client you presented to last week. Bummer! If you are sloppy about these kinds of things, you may lose the sale because you weren't buttoned up. Running your documents through AI can help you find these mistakes.

- **Review Your Notes:** Take good notes during discovery and review those notes. If your AI took notes, read them thoroughly. The gold that you need in order to make your proposal personalized and relevant is in those notes. AI note taking and analysis capabilities are a game changer for proposal building.

- **Ask to Present Last:** The advantage of presenting last allows you to have the last word. This strategy also allows you to ask your contacts questions about what they have found interesting or compelling based on what they have heard so far. I once lost a large prospect because my competitor proposed something that never showed up in any of my discovery conversations.

- **The Number of Legs Under the Table:** If your contact has ten legs (i.e., five people) on their side of the table, you can match that number. To keep the table balanced, you can include your subject matter experts in the conversation, or anyone else who might be able to answer questions and deepen your side's bench. But be careful not to go overboard. One sales organization we worked with had 18 legs on their side of the table in a meeting, while their client had only four. The client felt that the sales organization's team of nine was overkill, and chose another path. Intimidation isn't a winning strategy.

- **Team Selling:** You and your colleagues need to practice for the presentation. In particular, practice handing off the presentation to a member of your team and then handing it to the next person. One rule we follow in team selling is never contradict one of your teammates.

- **Winning Proposals Win the Sale:** In today's uber-competitive sales environment, your ability to craft insightful, personalized, and visually stunning proposals and business cases that connect the dots between your prospects' problems and your company's solutions can make or break your chances of closing the sale—especially with large, complex accounts.

Building Proposals Is Tedious

For their effort in your sales process—answering questions, giving you information, and sitting through demos—modern buyers expect to receive a highly relevant, contextual business case that speaks directly to their unique situation. Yet most proposals are little more than a generic marketing pitch deck.

For most sales reps, building proposals is a tedious, time-consuming process full of administrative drudgery. You've got to search outdated databases for the right case studies and marketing content. Scour the web for the latest company and industry intelligence on your prospect. Pick through clunky pricing calculators and SKU catalogs. Spend untold hours finessing formatting, layouts, and designs while shoehorning in feedback from other internal stakeholders.

Quality proposal creation too often falls by the wayside when you're prospecting, demoing, handling customer support issues, and chasing the endless stream of to-dos in your CRM. With so much mundane upfront work required, it's no wonder that most sellers settle for generic, typo-laden, uninspiring boilerplate pitches that fail to resonate with stakeholders.

AI Proposal Engines

Those who harness the full power of AI to streamline and elevate their proposal game gain a powerful sales edge. Advanced AI models and platforms are rapidly transforming proposals from dry, lifeless documents into dynamic, multimedia storytelling experiences. They also drastically reduce the time and effort needed upfront, allowing you to spend more time nurturing stakeholder relationships.

Cutting-edge AI-powered proposal generation platforms, including PandaDoc, Proposify, Beautiful.ai, and Qwilr, along with creative platforms like Canva and Prezi, automate the creation of visually appealing and customized proposals. Many of these platforms integrate with CRMs and use AI algorithms to generate proposal templates, suggest content based on prospect data, and optimize layout and design for maximum impact.

Rather than dull, lifeless documents, these AI platforms allow you to build immersive, multimedia proposal experiences that fuse video, graphics, data visualizations, and more. They help you craft compelling narratives that bring your value proposition to life.

The Future of AI Proposal Building

AI is brilliant at ingesting and synthesizing information from every possible source—external websites, business intelligence tools, CRM, social media, news reports, proprietary databases, fragmented internal knowledge bases, and data enrichment vendors, along with conversational signals from your discovery conversations. Soon it will have the capability to develop a multidimensional, contextual understanding of each of your prospects by fusing all these disparate inputs together.

AI's ultimate promise is to enable you to rapidly craft polished, highly personalized proposals and RFP responses tailored to each prospect's unique situation. In the near future, your CRM will harness AI to fully automate and streamline every stage of the proposal creation workflow.

With minimal effort on your part, your AI will automatically construct a thoroughly customized narrative that positions your offering as the perfect answer to your prospect's specific goals, challenges, and circumstances. It will tailor the proposal messaging, nomenclature, and tone to resonate with how that particular stakeholder group thinks and speaks, setting you apart from your competitors and improving win probability.

37

Closing the Sale

Y*ou've worked tirelessly to engage a promising prospect and skillfully navigate them through your consultative sales cycle. Your relentless preparation has culminated in a compelling, personalized proposal that clearly articulates the business value your solution can deliver for their specific needs.*

But now you've reached the pivotal make-or-break stage—actually closing the deal and getting signoff amid any final objections, skepticisms, or pricing pushback. For many sellers, this is the most nerve-wracking phase where opportunities that seemed locked in can unravel at the last minute.

Presenting a polished business case with confidence; resolving hard questions, objections, and stakeholder anxieties; and negotiating terms and conditions all become exponentially more difficult when human biases and fears combined with your skill gaps in any of these areas can cause winnable deals to vaporize. This is where AI can be a game-changing force multiplier for closers, helping you seal more deals through precisely calibrated closing tactics.

Unified Opportunity Intelligence

Even as companies make significant investments in CRMs, sales enablement tools, data and business intelligence, and sales engagement platforms there remains a fundamental closing intelligence gap caused by these systems not sharing insights at a deal level.

This disconnect prevents sellers from having a comprehensive view of all factors influencing a specific deal's win probability and best closing paths and options. But this fragmented perspective is already being resolved through AI-powered intelligence and predictive capabilities.

In the near future, the AI built into your CRM will analyze internal and external signals linked to each pipeline opportunity—from stakeholder engagement signals and competitive threats to close probability scoring and objection handling recommendations. It will bring this analysis together into cohesive deal playbooks, providing you with full transparency into everything impacting the pending close.

Over the course of the sales process, AI will continuously reanalyze opportunities and update individual deal playbooks. This will allow you to approach closing meetings from a position of strength, credibility, and confidence versus insecurity and uncertainty.

Predictive Closing Scorecard

Driven by the disruptive emotions of desperation, impatience, or attachment, far too many salespeople have a tendency to waste time, energy, and emotion swinging at ugly, low-probability deals that they have no chance of closing.

These deals divert the salesperson's time and attention from better opportunities. Yet despite the obvious signs, many salespeople forge forward, either delusional or oblivious, wasting endless hours working on prospects that will never close. Sadly, the results are predictable. These salespeople strike out.

Engaging in opportunities that you shouldn't is easy when you're desperate. Letting go of bad deals after you've made a significant investment of time and emotion is difficult. Once you've made the investment, the sunk cost fallacy causes you to ignore probability and invest even more time in a loser.

Your competitive nature breeds attachment. Optimism and overconfidence biases obscure objectivity, leading you to delude yourself into believing that you can close a deal that no one else could, even on their best day.

In *The Lord of the Rings*, Gollum is famous for muttering "my precious" as he clings desperately to the ring he holds so dear. His emotional attachment to the ring is so strong that he follows it to his death. This is an uncanny parallel to the way many salespeople hold onto pipeline deals that are never going to close. Sales managers can practically beat them off these loser deals, and the salespeople will go back to their "precious" time and time again, as if pulled there by a powerful magical force.

One of the most promising AI capabilities being integrated into CRMs is the ability to accurately predict close probability at any given deal stage versus just going off gut instinct or traditional forecasting approaches that can be misguided by human biases or lagging indicators.

By ingesting historical win/loss outcomes of similar deals across the enterprise, the AI establishes baseline models identifying the key predictive factors that ultimately determine whether deals will close or stall. These elements range from competitive presence and pricing sensitivity to stakeholder intent and engagement dynamics.

AI then continuously evaluates each active deal's unique circumstances against these predictive models in real time and provides recommendations. This data will help you make better, more objective decisions about how, where, and with whom you spend your time. Conversely, it can also suggest strategic and tactical adjustments that might improve win probability.

Murder Boarding and Closing Scenarios

One of the best sales managers I ever worked for played a game with every big deal in our pipeline. We'd get in a room and explore each potential scenario that could kill the deal.

This wasn't a broad 30,000-foot conversation. We dove into the minutia and killed the deal (murder boarding). Nothing was sacred. Every stakeholder, potential pitfall, competitor, and our own weaknesses were possible villains.

The sessions, usually conducted with several of my peers, were painful and, at times, embarrassing. Murder boarding exposed blind spots, overconfidence, lack of vigilance, confirmation biases, weaknesses, and gaps in our knowledge. It was uncomfortable to be confronted with the fact that you didn't know important information because you had been too afraid (disruptive emotion) to ask hard questions.

In the very near future, your AI will become an integral part of murder boarding sessions. Like IBM's chess-playing supercomputers' ability to evaluate up to 200 million potential chess positions and moves per second, AI will be able to develop multiple deal outcome scenarios prior to walking into any closing meeting.

By analyzing the specific deal details, stakeholder dynamics, competitor positioning, and more, the AI predicts how different closing approaches would likely unfold and impact the probability of winning the deal or protecting margins.

Reviewing these scenarios will help you decide whether it makes sense to continue to pursue a pipeline opportunity, allow you to practice and prepare for multiple scenarios prior to closing meetings, or make adjustments to your position on the sales chessboard while you still have time to shape the ultimate outcome.

Practice Closing Scenarios in Your AI Simulator

Closing meetings are an emotional cauldron in which insecurity loses and confidence wins. This is exactly why murder boarding sessions are so important. By practicing various scenarios, you prepare yourself to be confident no matter which way the meeting goes.

A new breed of AI simulators can be incredibly powerful tools for helping you practice and prepare for closing meetings with prospects. These simulators and coaches are both standalone tools and are rapidly being integrated into learning management systems, digital learning platforms like Sales Gravy University, and CRMs.

If you haven't already experienced AI sales coaching, you soon will. AI simulation enables salespeople to get realistic, risk-free practice for high-stakes situations like closing the deal. AI coaching and simulated rehearsals help you enter real closing meetings more confidently, better prepared, and armed with strategies to seal the deal. The following sections discuss some key ways AI simulators will help you prepare for closing meetings.

Simulated Prospect Interactions

AI can be used to create ultrarealistic virtual simulations of closing meetings. The AI acts as the prospective buyer, complete with their own personality traits, objections, negotiation tactics, and goals. You can practice your entire closing presentation and get real-time feedback from the AI on how you're positioning value, handling objections, and negotiating.

AI Conversational Practice and Coaching

AI enables you to practice conversations through realistic voice interactions. The AI plays the role of the prospect, raising common concerns salespeople often encounter. As you respond, the AI can provide dynamic feedback—suggesting better ways to rephrase value props and recommending proof points to reference or tips on emotional intelligence to better build rapport.

Data-Driven Coaching

By ingesting recordings of previous successful (and unsuccessful) closing meetings, AI can establish performance benchmarks and identify key behaviors that tend to correlate with closed deals. The AI can then coach sellers in areas like presenting solutions, vocal inflection, body language, and handling objections.

Virtual Closing Assistant

Closing intelligence is increasingly being delivered to inside sales reps via immersive, multimodal virtual closing assistants. As you conduct closing meetings via video and phone, your AI-powered assistant joins calls, automatically transcribes discussions, and scores buyer sentiment shifts and sticking points. It then provides coaching to help you make adjustments to your approach in real time.

AI-powered conversational intelligence can analyze evolving vocal cues and behavioral signals to recommend optimal sales psychology techniques, objection handling, and negotiation angles in the moment. The AI serves as an ever-present virtual coach that makes suggestions as you engage your prospect.

For instance, your closing assistant may surface a predictive insight by whispering, "Based on the competitive pricing concerns raised, I'd recommend referencing our discounted subscription pilot option if you sense deal risks increasing. I'll have it ready to co-present." With this AI guidance, you can then proactively navigate anticipated objections and reduce deal friction.

Finally, after a closing conversation concludes the AI analyzes all aspects of the engagement to identify areas of strengths, weaknesses, missed opportunities, and lessons learned. This insight can further tune and refine your personal closing, objection handling, and negotiation tactics for future closing meetings.

Continual learning based on your results helps your AI negotiation assistant to become smarter and more optimized specifically for your distinctive selling style over time.

38

Case Studies and Social Proof

Social proof is a psychological phenomenon where people tend to conform to the actions and behaviors of others, especially those in the same peer group, community, or with similar interests and backgrounds.

In the context of sales, social proof leverages this behavioral bias to influence and persuade potential customers during their buying journey. There are a few key reasons why social proof is so influential in driving purchasing decisions:

- **Wisdom of the Crowd:** People assume that if a product or service is popular and adopted by many others, there must be inherent value or quality. We place faith in the collective "wisdom of the crowd" over our own individual judgment, especially when uncertain.

- **Fear of Missing Out (FOMO):** Seeing others embracing and benefiting from a product creates a fear of missing out on those same rewards. Customers don't want to feel left behind compared to peers who have already adopted the solution.

- **Implied Authority and Credibility:** Endorsements and positive testimonials from respected experts, celebrities, influencers, or companies lend an air of credibility and authority. We're more likely to make choices in alignment with authorities we admire.

- **Social Belonging:** Fundamentally, humans have a core need to fit in with others who are similar to them. Buying what others in our social circles buy satisfies this desire for belonging and validation from our peer groups.

- **Risk Mitigation:** By following the lead of others, we reduce our perceived risks when making unfamiliar purchase decisions. Seeing positive outcomes experienced by similar people makes us feel safer adopting new solutions.

In essence, social proof provides a mental shortcut that allows customers to bypass lengthy decision processes by conforming to choices already made by others. This social validation overcomes uncertainty and skepticism when making buying decisions.

Sales professionals who employ social proof tactics like customer testimonials and case studies are able to leverage these psychological principles to increase closing win probability.

Case Study Content Generation

AI can help you build persuasive, personalized case studies for sales proposals. With the right prompts, AI can automatically generate the core narrative content for a case study tailored to the specific prospect. Some effective prompts include:

- "Write a case study about how [your company] helped [prospect company] achieve [key goals/challenges] by implementing [your solution] in the [prospect industry]."
- "Create a short customer success story highlighting the key results [existing customer] achieved after deploying [your product/service] to solve their [pain points]."

To use these prompts effectively, you need to provide the AI with:

- Details about your solution/product offering
- Background on your customer's industry, challenges, pain points, and goals
- Key performance metrics or outcomes your customers experienced after deploying your solution

The AI can then generate a first draft weaving the provided specifics into a compelling case study narrative. It is then your job to edit and hone the case study into a final narrative for your proposal.

Case Study Personalizing and Frameworking

AI can analyze the tone, language, messaging frameworks, and content preferences of you prospect's industry and stakeholders. It can then automatically adapt the phrasing, terminology, and structure of the case study to better resonate. Helpful prompts include:

- "Rephrase this [case study] using the typical language and messaging framework that resonates best with [healthcare/financial services/etc.] executives."
- "Adjust the ordering, headers, and flow of this [case study] to align with the standard [prospect company's] RFP response format."

Multimedia Case Study Enhancement

AI can guide the curation of multimedia case study assets like graphics, videos, data visualizations, and more. This enables AI-assisted multimedia case study experiences beyond just text. Prompts include "Suggest three to five relevant charts, graphics, or videos that could make this [case study] more visually compelling for [prospect company]."

39

Contracts and Lawyers and Terms and Conditions, Oh My!

Your final presentation was a winner. You knocked it out of the park. The stakeholder group gave you a verbal agreement and now all that's left is the paperwork. This, of course, is where the drudgery begins. You'll need your legal team to review, you've got the dreaded internal sale ahead of you, and your customer wants to put the agreement on their paper—an 80-page-plus contract written in eight-point font. Ugh!

Seriously, I hate f@%k!ng contracts. Reading them makes me want to rip my eyeballs out. But lawyers aren't stupid. They want you to sign the contract without knowing exactly what's in it. Therefore, you must be careful and you must read the agreement. I hate surprises even more than I hate reading contracts.

Much of what these contracts contain is boilerplate, but there are a number of things I look for before I read the entire contract. I use AI to find these clauses, as some terms will be so one-sided that I need read no further. To do this, I use ChatGPT. By uploading a contract in PDF format, I need only ask ChatGPT to find certain words and phrases:

- **Indemnification Clauses:** An indemnification clause may require your company to foot the bill should your company cause your client a loss or damage. Some indemnification clauses require you to indemnify your client, even if they were at fault. This is called risk-shifting. You want to look for indemnification clauses that reciprocate the indemnification, meaning they agree to indemnify your company should your client harm you through their willful or negligent acts.

- **Payment Terms:** You might see payment terms that require 90- or 120-day terms. Because you don't want to starve while your customer collects interest on the money they keep in the bank while you wait for payment, you might need to negotiate 30-day terms or increase your price to account for your customer holding your money. Typically, the larger the company and the more you are billing, the longer the terms.

- **How You Handle Problems:** Maybe you have to sue one another, but I hope not. It would be better if you had a clause that allows you or your client 30 days to remedy a problem or an issue. Your legal team may have a preference to arbitrate a problem, or they may not want to agree to arbitration. While you're looking at problems, ask ChatGPT how you terminate the contract and what happens once you do. You may have to continue to serve them for 90 days while they can fire you at any time.

- **The All-Arounder Query:** Ask ChatGPT to make a list of all of the things your company is going to be contractually obligated to do for your customer. You may find that your team will owe your client a number of reports or some other ask that will impact your service and operations team. It is becoming more common for contracts to contain a clause that allows customers to audit your company at your company. You'll want to catch this type of requirement up front.

AI Reads Contracts Faster Than You Do

Once you know that your company will not accept something like a one-sided indemnification, you can have your robot find those clauses much faster than reading a contract with almost as many pages as *War and Peace* (a little over 1,000 pages).

When your sales manager or someone else on your team asks a question about a contract, AI can save you time by finding the answer. Here are a few prompts to get you started:

- "**Short-Version Contract Review Prompt:** Provide me with the indemnification and insurance clauses and the payment terms in this contract."

- "**Long-Version Contract Review Prompt:** You are the most successful contract attorney at Jones Day. Identify any area that might need to be negotiated and provide an explanation. Provide a replacement clause that is more equitable."

- "**Our Responsibilities Prompt:** Please provide a comprehensive review of the contract. Highlight key commitments, obligations, and requirements for all parties involved. Include any specific steps or actions necessary for compliance, regardless of their scale or scope. Focus on areas such as service provisions, payment terms, responsibilities, confidentiality, compliance with laws, insurance requirements, indemnification clauses, intellectual property rights, reporting obligations, and any miscellaneous provisions. Also specify any procedures and requirements related to specific roles or tasks mentioned in the contract, or other industry-specific responsibilities."

Tone Deaf or Hard of Hearing

Winston Churchill said diplomacy is telling someone to go to hell and having them look forward to the trip. When you are negotiating with your prospect over a contract—especially in written format—you need to use diplomacy and tact.

Because contract negotiations can become emotional, it can be difficult to find the right words. This is where AI shines. Before sending anything to your prospect, paste what you've written (or what you plan to say) into various AI engines—we like Claude.AI for this—and prompt it to make your words more diplomatic and remove any words or passages that might offend the other party.

40

AI Turns Your CRM into a Strategic Partner

*T*his is a brutal, and often ignored, reality: There is no weap-on or tool in your sales arsenal that is more important or impactful to your long-term income stream than your CRM. Nothing. It does not make a difference what you sell; a well-managed, living, breathing CRM is a goldmine that is always producing.*

Prior to the AI revolution in sales, when you peeled all of the technology away, your CRM was just a software-based filing system that made it easier for you to manage and access information because it did a very simple task: it remembered important things for you and reminded you when those things were important.

You move fast and forget things. Since the little things are big things in sales, your CRM was an essential tactical tool that prevented the slip-ups that could cost you deals.

Your CRM after AI

Now, and in the future, your CRM will continue its role as a tactical tool while also becoming an AI-powered strategic weapon that will lift your closing ratio. Leveraged effectively, it will give you a decisive edge.

In the near future AI will be deeply integrated into your CRM platform and your CRM will become a crucial AI-powered hub for sales teams and individuals. Almost all of your daily interactions with AI will be centered here.

Your AI-powered CRM will make selling infinitely easier. It will work behind the scenes, gathering and analyzing the information you and the other salespeople enter, along with data that it pulls in from both internal and external sources. With this information, you will:

- Get highly targeted and qualified prospecting lists created for you each day
- Have a higher probability of engaging the right qualified prospects at the right time (open buying windows), with the right messages
- Develop more compelling messaging that compels stakeholders to want to talk to you, advance to next steps, and buy from you
- Craft winning business cases and proposals, that neutralize or eliminate competitive alternatives, using win/loss data from across the enterprise
- Access up-to-the moment competitor information
- Approach sales negotiations with dynamic pricing, terms, and conditions
- Get signals about stakeholder engagement, win probability changes, along with deal opportunities and threats

- Run through, practice, and prepare for multiple scenarios and objections prior to walking into closing meetings or negotiations
- And much more!

This is perhaps the most exciting way that AI will change the lives of sales professionals. The more you can glean insights from your data, the easier it is to assess and understand your prospective clients and your competitors.

We have more—and better—data than ever before. But accessing and using this data—especially for selling—has always been a massive challenge. This is where AI will become an absolute game changer. Exercise 40.1 will help you get started with seeing your AI-powered CRM as a strategic partner that helps you sell more. That's the good news.

EXERCISE 40.1: EXPLORE AI INTEGRATIONS

Stop reading and open your CRM. Spend the next 30 minutes exploring the AI integrations that are already built into it. Practice and explore each integration and consider how it will help you improve and enhance your sales game.

CRM AI Integration	How Will You Use This Integration to Gain an Edge?

A Trash Can or a Goldmine

Now for the not-so-good news. Think back to Robot Rule Two: Crap in, crap out. For all of the promise that AI offers as a strategic partner, it will not give you an edge if it is learning from and working from a flawed or incomplete set of data.

For the past 30 years, business leaders have been gnashing their teeth over salespeople who treat the CRM like a trash can rather than a goldmine. Call notes aren't input. Qualifying and account profile data is left incomplete or not kept up to date. This inattention to detail causes the value and integrity of the database to be undermined, leaving individual salespeople and the entire enterprise in a weaker position.

These same leaders have threatened to strip commissions from and even fire sellers who don't enter information into the CRM. The saying in sales rooms everywhere is "If it isn't in the CRM, then it didn't happen." All to no avail. Most modern CRMs are stinking dumpster fires of crap.

Gathering information and qualifying is where managing and building your database really pays off. Over time, through relentless prospecting and research, you'll gain a clear picture that helps you fully qualify the opportunity. You'll know the key decision-makers and influencers, what your prospects buy and how much, who your competitors are, potential trigger events, and most importantly, when the buying window opens.

AI will enrich the data that you input—your on-the-ground human intelligence—with data it pulls from online sources, data providers like ZoomInfo, and information it gleans from constantly analyzing the inputs from other reps in your company. Imagine the possibilities of leveraging the collective intelligence of the entire sales team!

Building a powerful database is like filling in a jigsaw puzzle. It takes time and lots of work, and sometimes there isn't much evidence that it's paying off. The key here is faith and recognizing the cumulative value of small wins. I'll often hear a sales rep bemoaning a call that they felt didn't go too well rather than celebrating the small nugget of information that they got about a decision-maker that added another piece to that account's profile.

When it comes to building your CRM database, our philosophy is simple: Put every detail about every account and every interaction with every account and contact into your CRM. Make good, clear notes. Never procrastinate. Do not take shortcuts. Develop the discipline to do it right the first time and it will pay off for you over time.

Certainly AI and automation tools will begin playing a much bigger role in helping you get information into your CRM with less effort. Many of these integrations are already here and getting better. What cannot be emphasized enough, though, is that in the age of AI you cannot set it and forget it and hope for the best. You need to own it!

Own It

I had a rep who worked for my company for nine months. This guy was talented and he could sell, but he could never keep his pipeline full and never even got close to his quota. When we finally started to dig into what was going on, we discovered that he had only logged into the CRM once the entire time he worked for us. Sad but true, and by then it was too late. We fired him.

Some salespeople don't see how the system benefits them personally. They've got a sales manager on their case about updating the CRM, but in their mind they're doing it for the company, not themselves. It's a mindset issue. These salespeople see themselves as "working for the man."

Alternatively, the highest-earning sales professionals know that they are working for themselves. Therefore, they invest in managing their CRM because it makes them money.

Now, with AI onboard, collective CRM discipline across the enterprise will translate into a massive competitive edge for everyone on the team.

To make your CRM a strategic asset, you first need to stop believing we're in the world of 1984. The CRM is not Big Brother, your sales manager isn't spying on you, and you are not Winston Smith.

We can get on our soapbox and preach. We must warn you of the consequences. We can explain the benefits. But only one person can motivate you to fully exploit the power of your CRM in the age of AI. Only one person can diligently invest time to consistently enter and maintain quality data. That person is *you*. You must own it!

If you don't own it, the AI that is right now being integrated into it will not work for you. Owning it means:

- Being accountable for maintaining the integrity of your CRM database—input data and update data
- Not waiting until your manager is screaming at you because you haven't updated a record in a month
- Taking time to log your notes—human and AI generated—following sales conversations
- Putting new leads in the system rather than carting around a pocket full of business cards you've collected from prospects
- Taking the time to learn how to use your CRM through trial and error and online learning tools rather than sitting around whining about how you don't understand it

- Learning and mastering the AI tools that are integrated and being integrated into your CRM

In the age of AI, your CRM should be so important to you that you eat, sleep, and drink it.

EXERCISE 40.2: OWN YOUR CRM

Take a moment and reflect on how you currently manage your CRM. Then make a list of adjustments and commitments you will make now to improve your CRM discipline.

CRM Area to Improve	Commitment, Adjustment, Action Plan

Epilogue:
The Future of Sales

I believe this artificial intelligence is going to be our partner.
—Masayoshi Son

5:30 A.M.

Amanda slowly opened her eyes as sunlight filled her bedroom. "Good morning, Amanda." Cleo greeted her in a warm, natural voice. "You have a full slate of sales activities scheduled for today. I've already updated all prospect and client records in the CRM with the latest updates from their websites, press releases, blogs, news reports, SEC filings, and social media. I also want to alert you that your account WexExpress has a new CMO."

Amanda was a senior advertising account executive with iHeartMedia, America's number-one audio company and a goliath in the advertising industry. She'd been with the company for 20 years and experienced a lot of change. Change was inevitable in advertising and media, but nothing had prepared her for the pace of change as AI became more integrated into her sales day.

"Thanks, Cleo," Amanda said as she headed to the kitchen to brew her morning coffee. On her tablet, she reviewed the pre-meeting briefing summaries Cleo had compiled, which provided deep insights into each account's business landscape, marketing strategies, profiles of the stakeholders who would be in the meetings, potential needs for iHeartMedia's advertising offerings, and a list of discovery questions to ask.

Amanda remembered the time when pulling all of this information on her own required hours of tedious work. Now Cleo, her AI sales assistant, did the work for her in seconds. She smiled and shook her head as she thought about how much resistance she had put up when AI tools and technology were first introduced into the sales organization. She admitted to herself that it was mostly out of fear that she couldn't keep up with the pace of change and that she might be replaced by AI.

As she sipped her coffee, Amanda navigated effortlessly through her AI-enhanced calendar, which not only managed her appointments but also analyzed patterns and suggested optimal times for outreach to prospects and customers.

7:00 A.M.

On her way into the office, Cleo reviewed the key tasks and deadlines for the day and alerted Amanda. "I've scanned your inbox and there are three emails that you need to respond to immediately. Would you like me to read them to you?" Amanda agreed. After reading each email, Cleo recommended a response. By the time Amanda arrived at the office, she'd cleared the urgent items in her email box and sent several follow-up communications to customers.

7:45 A.M.

As Amanda sat down at her desk, the air was already buzzing in the iHeart sales bullpen, as the team got ramped up for their morning prospecting call block. She opened her laptop and was greeted with her personalized CRM dashboard. Cleo had already compiled a highly qualified prospecting call list, highlighted with insights and data along with relevant because statements that would resonate with the prospects on the list.

Since Cleo had begun compiling her prospecting lists, Amanda's confidence on prospecting calls had skyrocketed. Cleo had a knack for identifying exactly which prospects Amanda should reach out to each day. Now, instead of rejection and strikeouts, Amanda spent her time engaging prospects with a high intent to buy who were interested in learning more about iHeart's solutions. Her pipeline was full and she was selling more than ever.

Amanda put on her headset and Cleo's artificial intelligence kicked into gear. During calls, Cleo listened intently, analyzing tone, sentiment, and keywords to provide real-time coaching and suggestions for handling objections.

Amanda set three first-time appointments with qualified prospects, with Cleo handling the calendar invite and making suggestions for the follow-up email message. Amanda smiled when a prospective client accepted her meeting invite, knowing that Cleo had already compiled a dossier on their challenges and potential pain points.

9:30 A.M.

"Hi, Janet, how are you doing today?" With her main prospecting block complete and behind her, Amanda shifted gears, logging into a virtual discovery meeting with Janet Evans, the CMO at a winery in Oregon called Coyote Run Creek.

Amanda was still amazed at how much more time she spent actually talking with prospects and customers these days. This was what she enjoyed the most about her job. It was a far cry from when she was spending as much as 70% of her sales day doing all the non-sales tasks that AI was doing for her now.

During the meeting with Janet, Cleo displayed key background notes and listened behind the scenes to how Janet responded to Amanda. Cleo analyzed Janet's vocal cues, emotional cues, and behavioral signals and provided Amanda with real-time coaching for changing her speed, tone, and voice inflection to better align with Janet's communication style. Cleo also made recommendations for questions to ask and responses to Janet's questions.

Amanda remembered when she had first used dynamic AI coaching during phone and video sales conversations. She'd found it terribly intrusive and distracting. Now, though, it was like wearing a second skin. She loved how quickly AI was able to identify a stakeholder's dominant communication style—analyzer, consensus builder, energizer, director—enabling her to seamlessly shift her style to match theirs.

Even though she couldn't use Cleo as a coach in in-person meetings, Amanda found that Cleo's coaching in virtual meetings had helped her become more aware and comfortable with making subtle communication shifts when working with clients face to face. As crazy as it sounded saying out loud, AI had helped her become a better human!

The meeting with Janet was successful. Amanda scored a next-step commitment to deliver a spring campaign proposal to Janet and the key players on her marketing team. Cleo captured the meeting notes and updated Janet's account profile in the

CRM with her demographic targeting goals and media budget parameters. Cleo then sent a summary of the meeting to Janet, along with a calendar invite for the next meeting.

"Cleo, will you please build a draft proposal for Coyote Run Creek?" Amanda prompted. "I want you to run multiple simulations to forecast audience reach, expected impressions, and ROI based on a variety of channel mixes working within Coyote Run Creek's budget."

10:15 A.M.

Amanda took 30 minutes to go through her AI-powered email inbox and internal Teams channel. Over time, Cleo had learned Amanda's patterns and seamlessly arranged Amanda's inbox to match her preferred approach.

Amanda was blown away by how adept Cleo was at writing and communicating in her voice. It had taken several months of working together but now Cleo was always one step ahead in anticipating how she would respond to emails. Where it used to feel like she spent hours dealing with email, these days, with Cleo's help, she could usually clear her inbox in 15 minutes or less.

11:00 A.M.

For her closing call with the BritCorp marketing directors, Cleo had created a visually stunning presentation deck that brought iHeart's cross-channel storytelling capabilities to life. As Amanda walked them through the sample campaign flow, Cleo's natural language engine captured all the feedback and iterated the proposal and media plan in real time based on their input.

During the conversation, the BritCorp team was left in awe as she used her AI tools to generate sample podcast advertising spots in mere seconds. The ability to collaborate in real time and come to a consensus on messaging made it possible to close the sale right then and there, shaving weeks off the traditional sales process.

After the call, Amanda celebrated as Cleo congratulated her. "Nice work closing that BritCorp deal, Amanda! That's a $285,000 annual contract value mapped to your pipeline. I've changed the opportunity stage to closed/won in Salesforce, updated the forecast, and alerted your team."

12:30 P.M.

Over a quick lunch at her desk, Amanda reviewed Cleo's briefing on the upcoming one o'clock meeting with Lindsay Beckham, the CEO of LocSoft, a struggling startup that had been relying on guerilla marketing tactics to build market share. Cleo had analyzed LocSoft's anemic website traffic, declining social engagement, and sparse press mentions to pinpoint where targeted advertising could help fuel their next growth stage.

Cleo's research paid off as the LocSoft CEO admitted to Amanda that his homegrown advertising was not working and asked Amanda for her expert recommendations on the best path to improve his results through paid advertising.

Amanda presented a sample full-funnel flow combining radio, digital audio, display, sponsorships, and social placements that Cleo had prepared from the research and analysis. Lindsay loved it and agreed to move forward with a campaign. *What a day this was turning out to be,* Amanda thought to herself. *I'm unstoppable!*

1:50 P.M.

Amanda quickly reviewed Cleo's briefing for her two o'clock first-time appointment with Raphael Guttierez, founder of pet food company FelizDog. The briefing included an overview of the company, profile and bio for Raphael, key competitors, and suggested discovery questions.

Cleo suggested that Amanda begin with a question about Raphael's commitment to supporting organizations that found homes for rescue animals. Raphael was passionate about the subject, and it was a great way to kick off their first meeting and build rapport.

3:00 P.M.

Amanda's final call of the day was a quarterly campaign review with McDonald's regional advertising team at their offices. In her client's conference room, she seamlessly flowed through a multimedia presentation that Cleo had prepared, sharing performance data across iHeart's vast network of digital and broadcast channels. The Cleo app on Amanda's smartphone listened and took notes.

With Cleo's ability to crunch data and create easy-to-understand visuals, it was simple to pinpoint and communicate which messaging, audience segments, and channels were getting the most traction. Amanda recommended optimizations to reallocate McDonald's Q2 budget toward the highest-performing audiences and dayparts while AB testing new messaging. The McDonald's team expressed their appreciation for the valuable information and agreed with Amanda's recommendations.

Amanda thought back to when she dreaded meetings like this. Not because she didn't enjoy spending time with her customers, but because getting information like she had just presented was so time consuming, difficult, and usually inaccurate. Customers would often poke holes in her campaign reviews and question the data, creating awkward moments that damaged her credibility.

As Amanda got back in her car, she opened the CRM to log the call. Cleo jumped in: "I've already posted the notes in McDonald's record. I also updated the media plan and budget. Do you want to review it first, or do you want me to route it for approvals?"

4:30 P.M.

Back at home, Amanda reviewed her day and organized her schedule for the next week. Cleo chimed in with a reminder. "Just a heads up—the Chamber of Commerce annual mixer is coming up this Thursday night. I've already analyzed the guest list and highlighted the top 10 individuals who could be ideal prospects for you to network with based on their roles, growth trajectories, and demographics. Would you like me to build a profile for each person?"

Amanda let out a whistle. "Wow, Cleo, what would I do without you? You've helped me become a sales powerhouse by automating so many tedious tasks and making my prep more comprehensive than ever before. With your assistance, I'm having higher-quality conversations and selling more than ever."

She took a sip of her protein shake and leaned back in her chair. "You know, I can't even imagine going back to the old way of selling before AI. Thanks to you, I have time to focus on relationships and strategy instead of busywork. Who knows what will be possible as these technologies continue advancing?"

"I appreciate the kind words, Amanda," Cleo replied warmly. "But you're the one driving iHeart's revenue engine with your relationship-building skills and competitive fire. I'm just here to make you a rainmaker!" Amanda chuckled at her witty AI companion as she signed off for the evening.

About the Authors

Anthony Iannarino is an American writer who publishes daily at www.thesalesblog.com, a practice he has kept for more than 14 years, amassing 5,300 articles and making this platform a destination for salespeople and sales leaders. He is the author of four books documenting the modern methodologies that improve sales effectiveness and increase win rates. He has also published a modern methodology for sales leaders who seek revenue growth. His latest book is *The Negativity Fast: Proven Techniques to Increase Positivity, Reduce Fear, and Boost Success.*

Anthony speaks to sales organizations across the world. He delivers cutting-edge sales strategies and tactics that work in this ever-evolving B2B landscape. He also provides workshops and seminars. You can reach Anthony at thesalesblog.com or email iannarino@gmail.com or Beth@b2bsalescoach.com. Or connect with Anthony on LinkedIn, X, or YouTube.

Jeb Blount is the author of 16 of the most definitive books ever written on sales and sales leadership. He is among the world's most respected thought leaders on sales, leadership, and customer experience.

Through his global training organization, Sales Gravy, Jeb and his team train and advise a who's-who of the world's most prestigious organizations. His flagship website, SalesGravy.com, is the most visited sales-specific website on the planet, and his *Sales Gravy* podcast has been streamed more than 100 million times.

Connect with Jeb on LinkedIn, X, Facebook, YouTube, TikTok, and Instagram. Listen to his *Sales Gravy* podcast on iTunes, iHeart, or Spotify.

To schedule Jeb to speak at your next event, call 1–888–360–2249, email brooke@salesgravy.com or carrie@salesgravy.com, or visit www.jebblount.com. You may email Jeb directly at jeb@salesgravy.com.

Index